THINK LIKE A DECORATOR

THINK LIKE A DECORATOR

[To Create a Comfortable, Original, and Stylish Home

By Leslie Banker

Foreword by Alexa Hampton

RIZZOLI
NEW YORK

New York · Paris · London · Milan

To Mom, with love
and admiration.

TABLE OF CONTENTS

FOREWORD

I have had the pleasure to know the fabulous Leslie Banker for a lifetime. Our parents were friends before a time either one of us can recall. We went to the same school for many years. We saw each other winter and summer, in New York and on Long Island. Our daughters, too, ended up in the same class decades later; and we have even lived on the same block for the past twenty years. Most interesting for me, though, is that we each chose to follow in the footsteps of a decorating parent.

Leslie Banker's mother was the late Pamela Banker, for decades a constant force in New York's interior design world. After establishing her own firm in the 1960s, Pamela became an associate at the famed McMillen Inc. She later joined the legendary firm Parish Hadley as a principal designer before cofounding Pamela Banker Associates with Leslie in 1999.

Leslie has lived and breathed interior design her whole life and she even literally wrote the book on design and renovation, when she and her mother coauthored *The Pocket Decorator* and *The Pocket Renovator*, both published by Rizzoli. Importantly, she weathered the storm of her mother's passing and the reinvention and reorganization of her firm under its new banner, Leslie Banker & Co. She has done this all with equal parts enduring style, great taste, and good humor.

In this, her latest book, *Think Like a Decorator*, Leslie manages to enunciate all of the expertise that she has accumulated, absorbed, and lived all these many years—and she is still a young woman! She embodies a trove of institutional knowledge that spans two generations—time spent crafting and perfecting a profession that has become essential to our current lives. Neither modernist nor traditionalist, Leslie Banker is simultaneously an eternal student of and expert in American design.

—Alexa Hampton

OPPOSITE: A bedroom designed by Alexa Hampton for the Kips Bay Decorator Show House is a rich mix of color, texture, and detail.

INTRODUCTION

Years ago, my mother, Pamela Banker, and I sat down to write a how-to-decorate book. It was 1999 and I had just started working for her at her interior design business. I wanted to pick her brain about everything she knew about decorating. Where do you even start? The plan for the book was that Mom was the expert and I was the writer (and student), and together we would create a resource that would actually teach someone, me included, how to decorate. After several attempts, we realized that it was too big a subject to tackle, especially since I had very little experience with decorating at the time. We kept coming back to the terminology, and eventually we wrote *The Pocket Decorator*, an encyclopedia for designers and laypeople. We realized that was where we had to start.

I worked with my mother for thirteen years and, over time, I learned from her how to decorate. When she died in 2013, I decided to carry on her business for as long as it made sense. It wasn't easy at first, but the projects kept coming in and eventually I felt like it was mine. A few years ago, when we were moving offices, I found the notes from the original how-to book we had started to write. The notes, many in Mom's distinctive handwriting, had ideas for the outline, as well as musings on how the role of a decorator was similar to that of an editor.

I remember sitting at the conference table in the office, all those years later, reading through the notes and thinking: Now is the time to write the how-to book. As always, it would be with Mom's expertise and guidance, in the form of her notes

and all the lessons learned. I realized that her ideas about the decorator playing the role of an editor were extremely timely in today's world of information overload.

"An interior designer must play the role of editor in producing the result the client wants while maintaining style, balance, proportion, and good taste" is one thing she wrote. Being an editor on a design project is about knowing how to develop the story of the space and helping the inhabitants of the house live their fullest and best life. This book starts with the idea that the first step in a decorating project is thinking about your story in the space. How do you want to live?

In the following chapters we cover ways to edit and filter information to come up with a design plan that works best for you. There's so much information out there. You can have a selection of thousands of different sofas at your fingertips in seconds. This can be overwhelming. The challenges of decorating have shifted dramatically in the past two decades, and this book aims to help you focus and edit for the best result, whether for a big project or a tiny one.

We'll talk about finding your starting points and about what is essential for a home and living comfortably there. We'll consider how important it is to be flexible and confident when designing. Last but not least, we'll look at the idea of enjoying the everyday and being your own best stylist.

ABOVE: My mother, Pamela Sullivan Banker, at a debutante party circa 1955.

So, here we are. I finally wrote the how-to book. I did it with a group of amazing designers who have given valuable advice and tips for the reader along the way. I am so grateful to Nina Edwards Anker, Lilly Bunn, Alexa Hampton, Kirill Istomin, Corey Damen Jenkins, Katie Leede, Amanda Nisbet, Kristin Paton, Katie Ridder, Tom Scheerer, and Christopher Spitzmiller for taking the time to share their expertise and photos of their work.

I am, of course, also grateful to my mother, who set me on this path with a phone call in 1999 asking if I would help her set up her new office. Parish Hadley, where she had worked for many years, was closing its doors, and she was relaunching the eponymous firm she'd run previously. When I was growing up, I always said I would never be a decorator. When anyone asked if I would one day follow in Mom's footsteps, I replied with a quick no—but Mom was so passionate about interior design and dedicated to her business that the only way to really know her was to work with her, and that was part of the appeal for me. She had tremendous energy. She was always curious and could be difficult at times. She was a force to be reckoned with. In saying yes to helping set up her office all those years ago, I was really saying that I wanted to get to know her better as a person and to understand what she was doing all day. The decorating was secondary to me then, but I surprised myself by actually loving it.

If there's one thing I'd tell her now, it's how proud I am of what she accomplished in her professional life. I've come to understand it better since she died. She grew up at a time and in a world where women didn't have careers. She forged a trail and it wasn't always easy. In the fifty-year span of her career, she mentored so many young designers, created so many beautiful spaces for clients whom she cared so much about, and worked with countless furniture designers and tradespeople whom she admired greatly. I miss her, yet she has been with me every step of the way.

OPPOSITE, CLOCKWISE FROM TOP LEFT: My mother loved throwing a party at home, like this early birthday party for me in Southampton. My mom and I relaxing at home in Southampton circa 1977. Mom, tired and happy, after a long day installing a project. The publicity photo of Mom and me for *The Pocket Decorator*.

CHAPTER 1

KNOWING YOUR STORY

Every space tells a story. It's up to you to decide what that story is going to be. Will it be the story of a globetrotting family with young children? Or that of a retired couple living in a tropical place with their art collection? Or, maybe it's the story of an introvert who loves nothing more than retreating to a quiet space to read. The story your house tells doesn't need to be the humdrum reality of your current existence; it can be aspirational, a daydream, a hope for the future. Maybe your story is that of a glamorous Hollywood star enjoying her golden years with friends, martinis, leopard-print rugs, and lots of bridge games—even if you've never been on a movie set. Most importantly, whatever it is, it should be a story that makes you happy.

While the story of your home won't be printed in words across the walls, and no one but you (and possibly your family or design team) even needs to know the details, it is the first step in creating the vision that will see the project through. Decorators understand that knowing the story means knowing what you want. If you hire a decorator to help you, their role is to guide the process to completion while making suggestions and decisions that will develop the story by adding depth, character, and a sense of place—all while making the homeowner's voice and style shine.

OPPOSITE: Our library/dining room in New York has dark green velvet upholstered walls that came with the apartment and that we decided to keep. They make the room feel cozy and are great for acoustics. The colors in the framed tapestry inspired the color scheme used throughout the apartment.

Every space has a color story as well as an overall general story. The design of my first apartment started with the paint color Morning Sunshine by Benjamin Moore. I loved how it reminded me of a similar hue I had seen on a vacation in Mexico. I painted the ceiling pale blue, Innocence by Benjamin Moore. Pale blue ceilings are one of my favorite decorating tricks. They bring the sky into your home, making the ceiling feel higher and the space bigger. The slipcovers, floors, and trim were kept neutral inside the yellow cocoon.

The Story of My First Apartment

My first apartment was in the West Village in New York City. It was on the sixteenth floor of a modern building. It had very basic, original to the building, three- or four-inch-wide door casings and baseboards. The crown molding had a traditional profile that had obviously been added later and didn't fit in architecturally at all. My mother had lent me some old pine furniture. I had so many piles of old *New Yorker* magazines that I probably looked like a hoarder (maybe I was a hoarder). I was in my early thirties and had saved a little money. I was single, and my first book, *The Pocket Decorator*, was about to come out.

I decided that the apartment didn't reflect where I wanted to be in my life. If you walked in you would have seen pine furniture that said "country farm," piles of magazines in the bookshelf that spilled over onto the floor and that said "messy and cluttered," and a futon that felt sad and said "college kid." I wanted to be grown up, modern, stylish, and throw fun parties. I looked through photos in magazines (Pinterest hadn't been invented yet) and was drawn to a warm, modern look with clean lines and strong colors.

OPPOSITE: For my first apartment, I splurged and bought a dining table and chairs from Vitra. They have been well worth the initial expense; I still use all of these pieces today.

That was the story for my redo, which I did all by myself. I was an adult, after all, and didn't want help—especially from my well-known designer mother. This was my moment to shine, even though I had a limited budget. I gave back the pine furniture and removed the traditional crown molding. The original door casings and baseboards were ugly, but they would have been expensive to replace and didn't contradict my story. If they were modern, they were fine. I would paint them the same color as the wall to make them disappear.

To replace the old pine table that I had used for a desk, I had a contractor make a built-in desk and dresser with flat doors over them that could be closed when I had friends over. At Vitra I bought a Jean Prouvé Guéridon table and some chairs, which were modern and felt grown up. The futon went out the door, and I did gratefully accept a comfortable vintage sofa from my mother, which I slipcovered in an inexpensive white denim, along with two upholstered chairs that were hand-me-downs. I got rid of all the magazines, all the CD covers, all my old Benetton sweaters from middle school and never looked back.

The one problem I still faced was how to host a dinner party without having my bed on display. Since the bed was in one corner of the L-shaped studio, I had a curtain made out of muslin, which is the fabric typically used as a lining under upholstery. With the curtain drawn, someone could imagine there was a whole other wing to the apartment behind it instead of just a little nook that fit a queen-size bed.

The finished apartment wasn't going to be on the cover of *Architectural Digest*, but I was very happy with the result because it got me where I wanted to be and I didn't spend a fortune getting there. I credit the success of this early project with knowing from the start what the story was and having a vision of how I wanted to live going forward.

OPPOSITE: An unlined basic muslin curtain is used to divide the bedroom area from the living area in my L-shaped studio apartment. A simple shelf high up, painted the same color as the wall, adds storage and display space.

RIGHT: The living room in our Rhode Island house was inspired by similar rooms from my childhood: comfortable and conducive to social gatherings. Much of the furniture was inherited. The mix of patterns works because the scale and design vary, and the colors connect.

Dressers aren't just for bedrooms. This chest of drawers was my grandmother's and I wanted to use it in our house in Rhode Island. It was the nicest chest of drawers that I had, so instead of putting it upstairs in a bedroom, I put it in the dining room. It is useful for storing placemats, napkins, silverware, and tablecloths, and I even threw a few silver trays into the bottom drawer. A piece like this can be found at auction, usually at a good price, and is useful in many locations.

A Country House Story

I am now married with my own family. We have a house in Rhode Island—a small nineteenth-century summer cottage with a rambling layout and some ill-thought-out additions. We were fortunate enough to be able to spend a considerable amount of time there during the pandemic in 2020. It was during this time that I decided I wanted to do more to help solve the climate crisis. We also wanted the house to be more conducive to outdoor entertaining. So, going forward, part of the story of our house is that we are going to retrofit it with heat pumps and more insulation. We also decided that we wanted to rebuild the front porch on the house, which had been removed by previous owners, so that in the future we would have covered outdoor space to hang out with friends. Thus, the story of the house became that it will eventually be both a restored traditional New England summer cottage for hosting guests and as close to carbon zero as possible.

Now, everything we do at the house is filtered through this lens, even though we are years away from reaching the goal. When our gas-fueled dryer broke, I replaced it with an electric dryer.

OPPOSITE: The dining room in our Rhode Island house is painted Farrow & Ball Babouche. The dark candle sconces on the wall add contrast. The rug is an antique Oushak from my grandmother's house. The stenciled yellow vessels were my mother's; she tried to sell them once and I protested so adamantly that she gave them to me.

LEFT AND OPPOSITE:
We use our sunporch in Rhode Island as an office by day and dining room by night. The floor is painted Benjamin Moore Chili Pepper, which adds warmth. The table and chairs are from my first apartment, page 17, and work nicely in this very different country setting. A few good pieces can go anywhere with you!

A STUDY IN CONTRAST

Consider the contrast of colors in a room. Do you like having dark against light? Or do you prefer to have the colors be of similar values so they blend together for a more uniform feeling? Contrast can be created with furniture, art, the frame of a mirror, or even trimming on linens. If you choose a pale wall color you can bring in contrast with dark accessories. Or, conversely, you can have a darker wall with lighter furnishings and accessories.

RIGHT: The guest room in Rhode Island has two flowered patterns of different scales, offset by strong straight black lines on the linens. Note the tape at the bottom edge of the gathered dust skirt, an added detail.

Don't be afraid to embrace pattern, or combinations of patterns, especially if they further your story. The key to mixing patterns is to vary the scales so they don't compete. You can also mix up the type of pattern—a large-scale floral with a small- or medium-scale geometric, for example. Don't be timid when it comes to pattern—it can add so much to a design.

When the electrician was at the house to make that change, I reviewed with him the size of our electrical panel to check if there was room to add a hook-up for an electric car and an induction range when the time was right to do that.

This is my story now at this house, and it will probably take years to achieve it. We're going to have to change all the single-pane windows, and add insulation and solar panels. But all these decisions now will build on each other because we have a plan.

In the end, whether you are working alone or in concert with a designer, the ultimate goal is the same: to live your best life in the space that you have. If you love to cook, then the kitchen needs to be a priority. If having dinner parties makes you happy, then there needs to be space to do that, no matter how small your home. If you have kids, then there should be a place for them to do homework and an extra bed to have a friend spend the night. If you work from home, you need a quiet space. You need to think about what will make you and your family happy and successful and what you want from life. Make a list and develop your story from it.

OPPOSITE: In my bathroom in Rhode Island, I wanted to take a bath and feel like I was in the tropics. This wallpaper from Clarence House is like a shot of vitamin C in the winter. I mixed in big blue polka dots, which look to me like raindrops. That's my story for this bathroom: it makes me feel like I'm on vacation.

The Life You Want to Lead

Think about the life you want to lead in your space. It's time for deep thoughts! These ideas will directly impact how you design your house. If you want to entertain at home, then you need to make room for a big dining room table. If you don't like entertaining, then skip the big table and turn the guest room into a library. Here are nine questions to ask yourself:

1. Why are you considering changing your space? Those reasons should drive the design process.

2. Are you entering a new chapter in life? Look forward, not back. What is important to your well-being in this new chapter?

3. What will make you happiest in the new space?

4. Do you want to encourage or discourage having friends and family over?

5. Is time alone to recharge important to you? If so, then think about where you can do that in your new space. Maybe a chair in your bedroom by the window, or another perch away from the action in the house.

6. Do you love to cook and spend time in the kitchen? If so, try to make room for seating in the kitchen at an island or a table.

7. Do you have any collections that make you happy? If so, how can you use or display them?

8. Do you care about the home environment? Clean air and water? If so, how can you integrate that into the design?

9. What do you need to feel organized?

OPPOSITE: Designer Amanda Nisbet created this dining room for clients with a large family who entertain often. The mandate was fresh yet timeless and fun. The trim and rug were designed in tandem to play off each other at different scales.

OPPOSITE: Outdoor areas should be considered rooms. This dining table here in the garden at our house in Rhode Island is great for a simple summer lunch. **ABOVE**: An indoor/outdoor space like this greenhouse only needs a bit of candlelight to be magical at night. Solar shades keep it cool during the day.

CASE STUDY

My parents had a greenhouse behind their house on Long Island when I was growing up. But as much as my mother liked gardening in theory, she liked entertaining more. The greenhouse had a small kitchenette with a long table running down the center. It was a perfect spot for a dinner party on a summer evening—and guests could even stay the night in the attached potting shed, which she turned into a little guest room with bath.

TELLING YOUR STORY
with Amanda Nisbet

How do you think storytelling helps when decorating?

AN: The story is really the thesis statement. It helps you decide the intention of the space, so then you know where to go.

What advice would you give someone who wasn't sure what their story was or where to start?

AN: Think hard about how you want to feel in a room. Think about the intention of the space. Are you young and eager to have parties? Are you an older newlywed and finally realizing your dream of an elegant home?

In your own homes, how has your story helped shape the design?

AN: My story in my house was my parents had beautiful homes but I wanted mine to be not so precious. I wanted beauty and function not to be mutually exclusive. I wanted it to be beautiful and comfortable.

Do you have an example of a space you've designed that had a story?

AN: For my Kips Bay Decorator Show House room, I got a room with faux boiserie on the walls. The boiserie reminded me of the nineteenth-century paintings by François Boucher, Jean-Honoré Fragonard, and Jean-Antoine Watteau, which were provocative. So, I decided to make my room flirty and sexy. My story for the room was it was the home of a modern-day courtesan. The pink Positano fabric was going to fail or be a big success, and luckily it was successful. It was a louche room.

How do you avoid getting overwhelmed by the volume of choices available in furnishings?

AN: I look at a lot more than I need to, but that's just me because I love the hunt and then I feel like I've done my homework. Instagram is too overwhelming. I look for a little while, then I need to take a break. Inspiration comes from my head, so I need to step away. My advice is to stay true to your own voice. You have to turn off the noise and step away because we are so bombarded.

OPPOSITE: In this seaside home enjoyed year-round, Amanda Nisbet wanted to utilize seasonal elements; the use of the color lavender and oak paneling brings the outside in. The custom carpet design echoes the water. FOLLOWING PAGES: Amanda Nisbet's Kips Bay Designer Show House room in New York was designed to be flirtatious. Her Positano Pink Lemonade fabric upholstering walls with boiserie sets the tone, as does the soft, balanced color palette.

CHAPTER 2

FINDING YOUR LOOK

Now that you have con-sidered the story of your home, it is time to figure out what it is going to look and feel like. It is time to look outward at inspiring spaces and build a vision that you can articulate to yourself and to others.

Start by finding photos of rooms and places that speak to you. Then, the hard work will be studying those photos and being able to say what it is about them that appeals to you. Spaces evoke emotions, such as calm, nostalgia, or energy, and being able to identify the look and feeling you want your new space to have is critical for getting the result that you want. This next step is to take the time to educate yourself and know what you like and don't like so that you then are able to communicate your vision as you dive into your project.

Finding the Words

As you collect images of spaces you like, practice deconstructing what you see and saying to yourself, or writing down, what exactly you like about the space. Is it calming? Is it fun? Is it sophisticated? It's hard to talk about

OPPOSITE: A sitting room/guest room at a house we decorated on eastern Long Island. The vintage wicker chairs, rattan, stripes, and straightforward design lend the room a beachy casual vibe. The painting is by Jennifer de Klaver, the sofa bed is from Joybird, and the striped rug is from Dash & Albert.

FOCUS ON: THE WORDS

"For each client," says Katie Leede, "at the beginning of the project I give them an expandable folder labeled by layout with things like 'lighting,' 'carpets,' 'colors,' 'couches,' and a stack of magazines, two Sharpies, and I tell them to tear out sheets, open a bottle of wine, and use the Sharpies to circle things they like and write one word next to each about why they like it."

visuals, and not everyone has the vocabulary. "I don't know I just like it" is not enough. You need to be able to articulate what the photograph conveys to you. You might say: "This space feels sophisticated and serene—I like the clean lines of the furniture, the neutral and calming color palette, the texture of the shaggy rug, the shots of black that add contrast. I love the framed photograph on the wall of the beach scene, as I would think I was on vacation every time I looked at it."

To create a similar feeling in your space as the one seen in an inspiration photo, you don't need to buy the exact chair in the photo; instead you need to understand the vibe of the room and choose pieces and colors and textures that work together to be in sync with that feeling you want to create and the lifestyle you want to live. Dig deep, deconstruct the image, translate the feelings into words. Whether you are talking to a designer or designing for yourself, having a detailed description like this in hand is like paving the road to your destination.

Instagram Versus Reality

Keep in mind that there is a world of difference between seeing a space in two dimensions versus seeing it in three dimensions. The room you love in a photograph is a two-dimensional interpretation of the three-dimensional space. A good photograph of a room is about the interior design and decorating, but it also reflects the skill of the photographer and the styling. When you look at a photograph of a room, you shouldn't feel bad if your own house doesn't compare—that's like feeling bad if you don't look like you stepped out of a fashion magazine spread.

A small room may be incredibly cozy but virtually impossible to photograph, while another room might not be much to see in person but is transformed by styling and the angle of the photograph. During a photo shoot, furniture is moved around and tabletops are styled, and later things like light switches and plugs are airbrushed out. The photograph is itself a many layered work of art that conveys a dream and an ideal that you probably won't ever capture exactly, but that you can strive to capture in spirit.

The Power of the Past

I once asked an appliance salesperson how most people, if there's a choice, decide whether to get an electric or a gas stove. His answer was simple: People want what they grew up with.

Everyone is influenced by the house they grew up in. It may be that you want to recreate your childhood home, or it may be the complete opposite reaction—that you want something totally different. Maybe you have inherited pieces of furniture from your family and you have to decide whether you want to incorporate them into your space or you are ready to let them go. Maybe the

OPPOSITE: This client loves crisp lines and contrast. The chairs are white with clean lines; the banquette seat cushion is a deep blue in contrast to the white woodwork; and the tabletop is white, which makes the artwork, by Jane McNally Wright, and the pillows pop.

BACKGROUND PATTERNS

Patterns aren't just printed onto fabrics or woven into rugs. You can bring patterns into a room in a variety of subtle ways, from the inlay on a piece of furniture, to the layout of a brick or tile floor, to the swirl in a piece of art, to the channeling on an upholstered headboard. As you consider and design a space, think about how you can layer in not only bold patterns, but quiet ones as well.

RIGHT: We wanted to create a comfortable and beachy feeling for this room. With our client, we chose natural materials, including the sisal rug, the lamps that are like green sea glass, and the four-poster bed, which helps to fill the space. The artwork by Jill Nathanson finishes the room.

heirloom furniture feels like an obligation or something you're stuck with and letting it go will be the best thing you can do.

Either way, where and how you grew up will inform your point of view. When starting a project, it's worth thinking about this. Did you grow up in a simple house and long for something more luxurious? Are you proud of your Swedish heritage and want to incorporate that into your home? Was there a place you loved? Were your parents messy and all you want in this life is a clean uncluttered space? Dwell on this for a little while and think about how much of your past you want or don't want to bring into your space now. Go for a walk, take a bath, or just stare out the window and ponder it. Do you want your new space to look and feel like another place you've known and loved?

Building a Reference Library

Since my mother was a well-versed decorator, I have her rooms rooted in my memory as design references. However, anyone can build their own reference library of places that inspire them, whether they are memories of a friend's house, images on Instagram, snapshots from a vacation, or a visit to a museum. It could be a room from a movie; friends used to tell me that my parents' house reminded them in spirit of the house from the movie *The Royal Tenenbaums* by Wes Anderson: the closet filled with board games and the tent in the living room. It is important to look at rooms by iconic decorators and analyze them. Over the next few pages, I will walk through some examples of the work of designers, such as Ray and Charles Eames, Tony Duquette, Albert Hadley, Mark Hampton, Sister Parish, and architect Philip Johnson. We will discuss the look of each room and dissect what elements of the space go into creating that look.

OPPOSITE: A long vintage table with a handmade French light fixture and blue grass-cloth walls make this Long Island dining room ready to be used any time of day, even as a pretty home office.

MAXIMUM MAXIMALISM

1 This photo of Dawnbridge in Los Angeles, which was interior designer Tony Duquette's house and now is owned by Hutton Wilkinson, the creative director of Tony Duquette Studios, is maximalism to the max. I love the shade of green with the black-and-white floor. The trellis on the ceiling adds texture. The molding at the top of the wall is over-the-top. The green of the exterior is part of the design of the room. The shot of red from the hanging birdcage gives contrast. The curtains and welcoming armchairs are of the same fabric. The chandelier and the plants all have similar narrow and squiggly lines. The collection of birdhouses is interesting, not something you see every day. This room looks comfortable. It has so many layers, colors, textures, and elements, yet they are balanced and work well to create a unique space.

STREAMLINED MODERN

2 In Philip Johnson's Glass House, I love how the outdoors is part of the interior. The furniture is spare and placed intentionally. The tufting on the chairs, the pattern and warm color of the brick, and the pile on the carpet keep it from feeling stark. The tree inside connects to the trees outside and brings life into the room. I like how this is so modern and yet not cold. It is tidy without any clutter. I suspect in the winter it would feel cozy and warm compared to the outdoors.

MID-CENTURY MODERN

3 The Eames House in Los Angeles is iconic modern design. I love how it's a little messy in the best possible way. The books in the shelf aren't perfect and the plants are a little akimbo. It looks inviting. I love how the outdoors is a part of the interior because of the big double-height wall of windows. I love those light fixtures and think they go in almost any space. The white floor keeps it light and feels modern. The layered rugs and mismatched pillows on the sofa contribute to the look, which is comfortable and not too polished or formal.

TIMELESS CLASSIC

4 Albert Hadley's apartment in New York has clean lines and contrast in color and feels to me sophisticated and playful at the same time. The shape and proportion of the sculpture over the mantel repeats the shape and proportion of the fireplace. The zebra rug adds pattern. The walls have subtle pattern. The chairs are mismatched. This room is graphic yet warm and inviting. It is modern and traditional at the same time. Just look at those two chairs next to each other. It is spare, yet the wallcovering adds quiet pattern and texture and looks luxurious.

COMFORTABLE ELEGANCE

5 Sister Parish's summer house in Maine evokes a feeling of comfort, easygoing elegance, and a sense of fun—note the cockatoo high on the wall. The coffee table, made with natural materials, has a country look. The curtains are full, with a ruffled trim, and made with a fabric that mixes floral with a blue stripe. It's not too fussy. There are multiple patterns and colors and yet they all hang together in balance.

"This is the living room in our family's house in Southampton. The chairs originally displayed their patterned chintz and then my father slip-covered them in a white self-stripe for a more graphic look. This is where I grew up and my children grew up; it is our decorating mainstay."
—*Alexa Hampton*

SOPHISTICATED CHIC

6 This room by Mark Hampton is timeless and so comfortably sophisticated. It will never get old. I love the contrast of the chocolate brown walls and the white trim and furniture. The busts are classical but the room feels current. I like how the upholstered chairs don't match— because when you are confident you aren't worried about everything matching. I like the sculptural side chairs and the shape of the bookcase, with the bust in it, makes it feel custom and distinctive. The proportion of the bookcase is perfect.

CASE STUDY

My all-time favorite space is the pale yellow living room in my parents' house in Southampton from when I was little. When you look at this room, you might think it looks dated. When I look at this room, I think of the slumber parties I had in there, the *Grease* sing-alongs, the ping-pong table that my parents eventually put in where that dining table is, and how I spent so many hours playing ping-pong that I am now actually quite good at it. My parents often had friends over for drinks in that room, which felt festive, and on rainy days I played Monopoly for hours on the white shag rug, which felt cozy. I think about how Peter Fasano hand-painted that fabric for my mom, and I remember, in about 1976, when my mom took me along with her to his studio in a walk-up on Madison Avenue and about Ninety-First Street and how I loved spending that time with her "on the job." I have a peacock chair today at my dining room table because of those peacock chairs. I have spent my adult life trying to recreate this space and the fun times we had there, whether it's for me or for my clients. It's not that space exactly, but the spirit of the space and how we lived there. I bet it has something to do with why I painted my first apartment yellow.

Finding Your Look

Find your three favorite designers and study their work. Write down or say out loud what specifically you like about what you see. Choose three of your favorite photos. Start with broad strokes that address the feeling of the overall spaces, and then drill down to what the rooms contain:

1. How would you describe the overall feeling or vibe of the room?

2. Does the room look formal? Comfortable? Like a place in the country or a place in the city? Take time to really think about it. Who do you imagine lives there?

3. How do the elements of the room contribute to this overall feeling? If it looks like a place in the country, is that because it has pine furniture? Does the choice of fabrics contribute to it looking like a country house?

4. What materials do you see in the photograph? Do you see bamboo? Steel? Lacquer? Fur? Stone? Wood? Glass? Brass?

5. Is the furniture all modern or all vintage? Do you see brown antiques? Is the furniture a combination of styles? If so, are you drawn to a mix like that?

6. What is the palette of the room? Is it all neutral or all a saturated color? Are there white walls with colorful furniture or gem-toned walls with neutral furniture?

7. Are there patterns? If so, are they big? Small? Is there a combination of patterns at different scales?

8. What textures do you see? Are things shaggy or shiny? Or a combination of both?

9. Is the space cluttered or spare?

10. Are the lines of the furnishings straight or squiggly? Or a combination of the two?

11. Is there symmetry of furnishings? Or are things asymmetrical?

12. How many things are on legs and how many are solidly on the floor?

OPPOSITE: The house in Southampton where I grew up had simple white slipcovers, Parsons-style coffee and console tables, and hand-painted fabric pillows and ottomans. The peacock chairs could be moved over to the dining table for extra seating.

DEVELOPING A POINT OF VIEW
with Katie Leede

What advice do you have for people who are in the early stages of a design project?

KL: You have to develop a point of view, develop a voice. If you want to be a creative partner you have to understand who you love, what you love, and why you like things. People need to start with really studying first and foremost: Who are the designers that speak to me and why do I like them?

What should people ask themselves at the beginning of a design project?

KL: When you start a project you have to ask: Who is your ideal self? How does your ideal self live? What are the practical ways your best self lives? Is cooking important to you? Do you want to cook with your children? If so, what does that mean in terms of your kitchen and pantry? Do you want to play games, such as backgammon, chess, or poker?

How do you talk with clients about design?

KL: It's very difficult when people just say, "I know what I don't like." It's much easier when people know what they do like. Make it a fun game—ask them to look at something and say what they like about it. Talk about whether they have a favorite hotel that they have fallen in love with and why they like it. How do they imagine using the space? How do they live now and how do they want to live going forward? On the spectrum of traditional to modern, where are they?

What else is important when starting to work with clients on a project?

KL: Organization really helps. Where are the games going to go? How will you organize the games? People need to go into different spaces in a house, so will there be a workspace on the upstairs landing? You have to ask yourself how you will make every part of the space come alive and beckon. Asking the right questions is very important.

Where do you find inspiration?

KL: Traveling is a big source of inspiration for me. And books, especially books on old textiles. I am inspired by museums. I like the idea of taking yourself on little dates to think about what inspires you and what excites you. Go on artist dates with yourself—it could be to a fish store and you might be inspired by the color of the fish. You have to train your eye. Going out and looking and thinking about things gives you the input that you can use in your work and in your life.

What if something isn't working?

KL: Albert Hadley was known to take off his shoes and start moving furniture around a room. Sometimes just because you ordered something for a place doesn't mean it's going to live there. Hopefully it will be perfect, but it's important to be bold enough and brave enough to move it right around and see if it works better somewhere else.

OPPOSITE: In Katie Leede's SoHo loft, high and low intermingle seamlessly: a simple Prouvé light fixture hangs a over a vintage Portuguese farm table surrounded by comfortable chic swivel leather dining chairs of her own design. A CB2 shelving unit houses an inherited collection of Royal Crown Derby china. **FOLLOWING PAGES:** Another view of Leede's loft. The night-blooming cereus sprang from a single cutting taken in the 1920s from her husband's grandfather's plant.

CHAPTER 3

DROPPING ANCHORS

At the beginning, when a project is still on the drawing board, after you have thought about the story and found the look that you want, it is time to drop a few anchors. An anchor might be a paint color you definitely want to use, a non-negotiable item like a rug that has been in your family for generations, or a wood finish that simply has the right vibe. Anchors might be things that you already have and don't want to or can't afford to change, such as a stone floor or an existing wallpaper. These anchors are a starting point and will lead you into your schemes. They will guide your first foray into tangible samples and colors. The typical advice that decorators give is that when developing a scheme, you should start with the rug selection and work up from there. This is good advice, in that a rug gives you an anchor, a starting point, for the rest of the room to follow. However, there are many other elements that can be anchors.

I believe that every project starts with some anchors, no matter whether it's a tiny project or a major redo.

OPPOSITE: The panel on the wall of this New York apartment inspired the palette for the room; the raspberry-red chair and blue dots in the pillow echo its colors.

FOCUS ON: PAINT FINISH

Picking paint colors also means selecting the finish, or sheen. Ceilings are typically flat. Flat walls won't clean as easily as those with shine, but they have a nice chalky look. Eggshell has a slight reflection and is typically selected for kitchens and bathrooms. Baseboards, doors, and crown molding are usually painted in a satin finish for durability. High gloss is for a special wow moment.

Color

As you make plans, keep thinking about how different colors make you feel. While color theory may say one thing, ultimately how you feel about color is personal. Some colors (yellow comes to mind) are like the herb cilantro—certain people just have an aversion to them.

My friend Gretchen asked me to help her redo her apartment in New York, which I was thrilled to do. The first time I met with her about it, she told me that she loved the Benjamin Moore paint color Iron Mountain, a dark gray. She had seen it on the walls at a restaurant and asked the management about the color. She had seen it again in a magazine. It made her happy, and she had chosen it for the walls of her den, which needed to be repainted. The color was our anchor for that room, and we based the fabrics, rug, and window treatment selections around it.

The deep gray gave us a starting point and worked with Gretchen's story, which was that she wanted her apartment to feel refreshed. A lot of the furnishings were things that her parents had lent her when she had moved in years earlier, and the rooms were starting to look tired after about a decade.

After deciding on the Iron Mountain, we looked around Gretchen's apartment, continuing to talk about what the scope of the project would be. We were looking at specific things and discussing whether they should stay or go. The dining table and

OPPOSITE: My friend Gretchen's den is painted in Benjamin Moore Iron Mountain. The sofa is from Kravet and the rug is a Tibetan hand-tufted wool. The red armoire adds color, and the gallery of prints fills a long wall. Notice how we placed objects of varying heights on top of the armoire.

mirrors hung on the wall around it would stay; the living room sofa, rug, coffee table, and side tables—most of them hand-me-downs that were not making Gretchen feel happy—would all go. The living room rug had spots that wouldn't come out and wasn't, in my opinion, big enough.

On the walls in the living room were two large Chinese panels, one with a rooster and the other with two blue birds. The colors were beautiful and, as luck would have it, the deep grays in the panels worked perfectly with the walls in the den next door. We now had some synergy and a palette to work off of for the living room. We would pull the blues and reds from the Chinese panels into the furnishings, so those panels became another anchor.

Gretchen had a bentwood loveseat that she'd bought at auction. She'd had it re-caned and definitely wanted to use it in the room. Since there was really only one place in the living room for it, we would work the furniture plan around it. This was another anchor that informed the decisions going forward.

As you can see in the photos of Gretchen's finished apartment, the anchors set the tone and gave us great starting points. You wouldn't know what those anchors were looking at the photos of the finished space, but they got the process going.

Architecture

In another house on Long Island, the architecture itself was the anchor. The house had been designed by the late architect Charles Gwathmey. It had gone through significant renovations by previous owners, so there was some freedom to make changes to the architecture, as what was there was not all original. The story for the project was that it was a modern house by the ocean that needed to be updated and made modern again. The house was forty-plus years old and was due for substantial repairs and upgrades to suit a contemporary family. But we wanted to keep its modern spirit.

OPPOSITE: For a bedroom in a beach house on Long Island, there is a custom colored rug from The Rug Company, and the bed is walnut from Hudson Furniture. The lamp, linens, and art bring in color and detail to complete the room. The rug and its colors were the starting point for the design of the room.

While walls are often flat wallboard, they can also be clad in boards that run vertically or horizontally. This adds pattern and interest to a space. Wainscoting refers to paneling on the lower half of the wall, which is traditionally used for decorative or practical purposes, such as protecting the surface from scuffs or dings.

The furnishings would be streamlined to mirror the clean lines and curves of the building. In the first meeting we had about the interior design, I pulled out wood and stone samples, as well as a small pile of rug samples and fabrics I thought could work well in the space. I was basically throwing things at the wall to see what would stick. I was looking for anchors, a few things to start our process. We landed on a weathered looking teak sample, a sample of dark walnut veneer, and an ocean blue colored fabric that referenced the ocean just beyond the deck. Those things, paired with the white walls and light wood floors from the original iteration we knew we'd keep, were the anchors that got us started.

How did we choose those things? The client was simply drawn to them, and they fit the story and the look. Teak and ocean blue make sense for a house by the beach. The walnut created contrast. The combination of all these things together made us happy.

As you work, it's important to keep in mind what the story is and how these anchors work to support the story. In some cases, even after the design has been developed, it might be that something isn't working. That no matter how you try, the whole thing doesn't quite hang together. In this case, it's important to keep an open mind and be willing to let go of decisions you've made, even if you thought they were anchors in the project. Maybe, after all, that family heirloom rug just doesn't work in the space. We'll talk more in chapter six about killing your darlings. For now, keep in mind that decorating is a process, and choosing anchors will get you started.

ABOVE: A quiet mezzanine in a Long Island beach house looking out at the view. RIGHT: the samples that kicked off the design for the project. FOLLOWING PAGES: The living room incorporates a walnut media cabinet, custom dyed blue mohair rug, blue linen and walnut Holly Hunt chair, and sectional from Dune with ikat pillows.

WALLCOVERINGS

The walls and ceilings of a room don't have to be finished in paint. You could have wallpaper, a natural wood finish, a pickled wood finish, mirror, a polished plaster finish, or even an upholstered wall. There are some wallpapers that look like wood, adding warmth and texture to a room. When starting out on the design of a room, especially if it's a renovation or long-term home, consider all the options before jumping into painting everything.

RIGHT: Tom Scheerer designed this house on the water in Florida. The seating area is purposely oriented away from the water view for a cozier feeling. The sofa is a classic English style with fringe. Antique Chinese storage jars were turned into lamps to go on the side tables.

CASE STUDY

When we talk about non-negotiables, I love to bring up my parents' old dining room on Long Island. There was a column right in the middle of the room. My parents didn't want to go to the trouble or expense of putting in a steel beam to support the ceiling, so they instead decided to build a dining room table around the column. Sometimes creativity springs from necessity.

What Are Your Starting Points?

One place to start a project is by asking yourself what is non-negotiable and what your anchors are. Here are a few things to consider:

1. Do you have a set amount of money to spend? Is it going to be stressful if you exceed a certain number? If so, don't push it—make that number non-negotiable. Leave room in your budget, 15 to 20 percent, for the unexpected and things like shipping costs, sales tax, and accessorizing.

2. Is there a date by which you need to move into the house? If so, this will influence your selections and scope of work.

3. Look at the architecture. Is there anything that needs to change? This might include anything from renovating rooms, to changing crown moldings, to creating more storage space. These can serve as important starting points.

4. Is there anything you or your family must have to live comfortably? Private office space? Handicapped accessibility?

5. What pieces of furniture do you have now and definitely want to use? Start your furniture plans with these.

6. What parts of the existing design are you going to keep as is? The wallpaper in a bedroom? The stone floor in the front hall? Decide what you want to leave; this will help you focus on what you're going to change.

7. Figuring out your scope of work is an important starting point. What are you planning to do in this project? Just decorate? New doorknobs? New air conditioning? Total renovation? Before you can get budgets or plans together you need to have an idea of the work you want to do.

OPPOSITE: The floors of my parents' old dining room were Mexican terra-cotta; I loved how it had pawprints from an animal that must have walked across it while it was in the tile factory. The curtain pole is hung high to be level with the top of the small square window; this gives the room a feeling of height.

STARTING A PROJECT
with Tom Scheerer

Are there any questions you ask a client at the beginning of a project?

TS: It's important to establish the client's capacity for "decorating." Do they want a decorated look with emphasis on upholstery and fabrics (further layered with antiques and decorative objects)? Or more of a curated look emphasizing works of art and objects?

What are some of the first decisions made on a new project?

TS: All good decorating starts with a "corrected" architectural framework, followed by a strong furniture plan. Hopefully one that is not static and predictable. The furniture plan and flow of the room are tantamount to colors, materials, and even furniture forms.

Do you typically start with the rug when putting together a scheme?

TS: The simple answer is no—except in the case where a client may have a wonderful rug. I recently installed a taxicab yellow dining room, which worked wonderfully with a yellow and orange Oushak carpet from the client's former apartment.

What do you find essential to a well-decorated house?

TS: I rarely have trouble delivering a well-decorated house. It's a harder proposition to get the clients to know how to live in it. If the rooms are designed for comfort and variety, they can and should all be used well. I always think it's sad when clients don't derive pleasure from cooking and entertaining in the rooms we devise for them. Eating takeout sandwiches at the kitchen island is anathema to me. If you don't cook, you shouldn't have an island!

Where do you find inspiration for your work?

TS: Aside from my large collection of vintage decorating books (most pre-1990), I'm always soaking up atmosphere when I travel. Two years of trips to Sweden for a project left a lasting impression, and I also see trips to Japan and Greece percolating through my work.

Do you have any favorite tricks for styling a house once it's finished?

TS: Green plants everywhere. A room without greenery is often lifeless in more ways than one. And I don't mean cut flower arrangements or even orchids. A plant that can find a comfortable "successful" corner of a room can go on forever.

OPPOSITE: One of the two entrance halls in a waterside Florida house designed by Tom Scheerer is in the open air. The mirror and the table base were commissioned in India. The tabletop is Moroccan tile. Seashell sconces were made of Fiberglas and painted to match the Florida coral stone walls. The lantern was designed for the house by Scheerer. Its bulb is shaded by a glass cylinder to approximate candlelight. **FOLLOWING PAGES:** At the same Florida house, Scheerer's clients decided at the final hour to eliminate the formal living room, as it was getting too big! This furnished loggia takes its place and is suitable for outdoor living most of the year. (On cold nights an indoor library with a fireplace is used as a retreat.) The furniture, none of it specifically made for the outdoors, is protected from the elements by rolling shutters, concealed during the day, that come down at night after the clients go to bed.

LEFT: Tom Scheerer designed this Florida ground-floor study with dark brown walls and lavender, purple, and ultramarine color scheme. The rug is a vintage cotton and jute dhurrie and the desk was made in India. OPPOSITE: A breakfast room designed by Scheerer for the same Florida project has a custom-made camelback sofa and lamps made from antique pickle jars.

CHAPTER 4

MAKING A PLAN

The next step is to start thinking about your space in depth and what specifically your plan is for the redo. There will be your overall plan, and then there will be your furniture plan. Making an overall plan means deciding what the scope of work will be: renovations (if any), painting, wallpapering, new window treatments, and whatever else you will do in this project. The furniture plan will be a room-by-room layout showing where the furniture, including lighting, will go and what size each piece will be. In creating a furniture plan, you will consider what furnishings work best in the space to live comfortably, what you already have and want to use, and how it all will be arranged.

Start this process by studying your space carefully. Notice where the morning light comes in, what the best views are out the windows, where there is wasted space, and where it would be comfortable to sit. If you are redoing your space, think about what doesn't work about it now that you would change. Are there any unused rooms or corners? All this will inform your furniture plan, which is an essential part of any interior design project. It doesn't matter whether you have priceless antiques or a mix of IKEA and hand-me-downs—if the furniture plan is well considered the space will be functional.

OPPOSITE: This front hall has all of the essentials: a spot for keys by the door, a seat for putting on shoes, and a place to hang hats and coats. Simple but functional.

CHOOSING A SOFA

The design of a sofa will set the look for a room and inform how a room is used. Look at your inspiration images and note: How many seat cushions do the sofas have? I prefer three when possible. Are the seat and back cushions loose or tight? Loose is comfier. Does it have a skirt or legs? Are the arms high or low? Pay attention to seat depth: 28 inches or more is best for lounging, but a sofa that deep will require throw pillows for people to sit up comfortably.

RIGHT: A cottage in Connecticut we worked on has splattered wallpaper by Peter Fasano, an Elizabeth Eakins rug, and Katie Leede's Isis fabric on the throw pillows. The sofa on legs feels less fussy than one with a skirt.

A professional designer at this point would make furniture plans to scale, either drafted by hand or, more likely these days, using CAD (computer-aided design). If you are working on your own, buy a tape measure if you don't already have one and a roll of blue masking tape to mark the outlines of furniture on the floor, and track down any floor plans that might already exist of the space.

The Essentials

The best place to begin is with a list of the essentials for your new space. These are the basic building blocks that you need in your home to live comfortably. For example, no matter the budget, everyone living in a household needs to have a bed with a light next to it. There should be a table for meals that is big enough to seat everyone in the household at once (and guests, if entertaining is important). Everyone in the household, students included, needs a well-lit place to work. You need a place by the front door to hang a coat and put down a set of keys. You need adequate storage for clothes, shoes, and linens. These are elements that pretty much everyone will agree on.

From the very basic you can expand to things like having a variety of chairs, some squishy and some straight, in the living room, to accommodate everyone who might sit in a conversation grouping. Not everyone loves a stuffed chair, and someone who has a bad back may need a straight chair with a higher seat height. In every conversation grouping I like to have small footstools and ottomans for anyone (but especially kids) to pull up and move around. That is an essential item for me in my house.

The list of essentials will vary depending on people's budgets and lifestyles and what the story is for the space. If your story is

OPPOSITE: The old painted wood floors of the cottage were left as is. This cozy corner for reading has the essentials: a good light, a comfy chair, and a place to rest your feet. Chair fabric is Katie Leede's Kimono Negative.

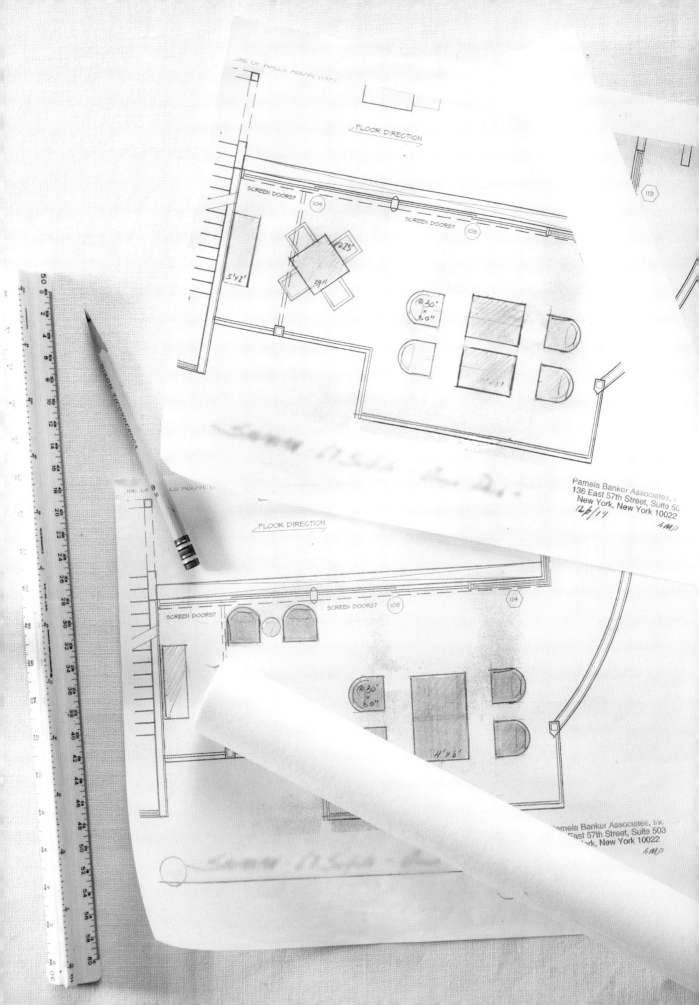

How to Make a Furniture Plan

A furniture plan starts with an empty floor plan of the space. Often you can get a floor plan from a real estate agent if you are buying or renting. There are also services that will survey your space and make floor plans, or you can get your tape measure out and survey the room yourself.

To do this, sketch the shape of the room, then measure each wall, noting where the windows and doors are, and any outlets.

Once you have the sketch with the measurements, redraw it to scale so that one foot of the actual space is represented by, for example, a half inch in the drawing. Having a scale ruler is useful for this. So, if a wall is 12 feet long, in the drawing it would be 6 inches. If another wall is 9 feet long, it would be 4½ inches on the drawing.

Once you have the basic shape of the room drawn to scale, draw in the furniture, making sure the scale is the same.

Start dropping your essentials into the furniture plan. Add the most important pieces first. For example, put the beds in the bedrooms, determine where the dining table will go, and do the same for the couch in the living room. Take time with the furniture plans. Move things around, and brainstorm ideas.

KEEP IN MIND THESE KEY POINTS:

1. In the living room, where will the sofa go? What is the sofa's optimal length, height, and depth? Do you want room for side tables or chairs on either side of the sofa?

2. In the bedrooms, what size bed fits? Is there enough space for bedside tables? How wide can they be?

3. Where will TVs go—in the kitchen? Bedrooms? What will go under the TVs?

4. Where will you have meals? What size and shape dining tables work best? How many people do you want to seat at once? Should you consider a banquette or built-in bench?

5. Where will desks go? Is there room in the bedrooms? Do you like having bookshelves? If so, where will those go?

6. Will your outlets work with the furniture plan?

7. Where will guests stay?

Remember, the best furniture plans allow for flexibility. A small chair to be pulled up or moved around. Upholstered chairs on swivels allow for flexibility if the TV isn't centered on the seating area.

If making a full furniture plan to scale is too much of a project, you can at least keep your tape measure handy and check the size of everything in the space. Using blue masking tape to mark where furniture will go will help you, for example, figure out if you need a 7-foot or an 8-foot sofa.

that you have a world-famous toy soldier collection, then it will be important for you to have shelves or some way to display the collection. Maybe you need an armoire for your bedding and towels if there isn't a linen closet. Someone may say that they can't live without a wine cellar, while someone else might simply need blackout shades in the bedroom to sleep well. Start with a list of what is essential to you and your family. You will start your furniture plan with these items.

Analyzing the Space

Once you've made a list of the essentials, it's time to study the space until you feel like you know it intimately. How will you be using each room? What is the view out the window? Which rooms get evening light? Where would you like to sit and have coffee? Spend time in the space imagining and brainstorming where you will sit, eat, and sleep. Plans that might have seemed logical can shift when viewed through this lens.

For example, in the bedroom of my apartment in New York, there is one big, long wall where a king-size bed would logically go. It's where the previous owners had their bed and where I thought we'd put ours. That is, until I stepped to the spot in the empty room where my head would go and realized that I would be waking up every day and looking into a big white apartment building across the street.

However, If I squeezed the bed onto the smaller opposite wall in the room, I would wake up every morning with a stunning view of the East River looking over Four Freedoms Park on Roosevelt Island. It was a no-brainer, and this informed my furniture plan. The room is a little kooky because of this, and yet I am so much happier living there. And it took spending time in the space to get there.

OPPOSITE: The walls of my bedroom in Manhattan are Benjamin Moore Cool Lava in a flat finish; the trim is Dragon's Breath. The color was inspired by a tapestry in our dining room (see page 14). FOLLOWING PAGE: The headboard is Jane Shelton ticking with a line of color to match the walls. The ticking is railroaded to run horizontally as opposed to vertically, which feels more modern.

Designers on What Is Essential

"The ability to sit comfortably. I need to be comfortable. In the most critical way, there needs to be good HVAC. You need to have a good mattress, lights on dimmers, and books. You have to have books."

—Alexa Hampton

"A pad and pencil next to the bed is essential. I learned that from Albert Hadley. The key to anxiety is moving through it, and making a list helps. Albert had pads everywhere that said 'Don't Forget!' The act of writing something down is so important. If you make a list and then forget your actual list, you'll still remember 70 or 80 percent of what was on it."

—Christopher Spitzmiller

"As a practical tip, I would say if you are on a budget to invest in a good piece of upholstered furniture. Almost every room requires a good piece of upholstery. Every living room requires a sofa; every library requires a chair. It could be very modern or very traditional, but it needs to reflect your own personal style. The fabric doesn't matter; it's about proportionally comfortable furniture that you can recover many times in many ways, but the bones of that piece of furniture will remain."

—Kirill Istomin

"Family photographs are essential. So is family art and personal things that can't be found at Target. A house should have something that is unique to you. To me, a house is not a home until you put in a personal element."

—Amanda Nisbet

"Lighting is so important. I could live on a mattress on the floor if I had a really good, cozy reading light next to me. I love brass reading lights because they make the light warmer. I also love sconces and candles, and solar lights, too; they have a warm soft glow waiting for you when you get home. Also, a really good storage cabinet that is beautiful and hides all your junk. And then a system in the storage cabinet so that you can find things easily."

—Nina Edwards Anker

DECORATING WITH PAINT

Designer Lilly Bunn painted all the trim in her Long Island cottage a Farrow & Ball dark green in the estate eggshell finish that she describes as the "big solution" to the space. The finish, less shiny than satin, helps hide the imperfections of the house including layers of paint in an old house that didn't have a straight line anywhere. A shinier finish would have highlighted all the bumps. Bunn liked the character of the old windows and didn't want curtains—the dark trim helps to make the windows look finished.

RIGHT: Designer Lilly Bunn's house in Locust Valley has classic Antelope carpeting running up the stairs, faux bois Nobilis wallpaper running horizontally, and a table by the front door that serves as the perfect spot for keys or mail. FOLLOWING PAGES: Bunn says that she purposely avoided having everything match in the living room at her cottage, because it makes it easier to add things over time.

PUBLIC VERSUS PRIVATE

At this point, you can now identify which parts of the house are public, like the front hall and the living room, and which are private, like the bedrooms. If there's a mudroom, is it going to be treated like the front, or formal, part of the house, or is it part of the back, or utilitarian, part of the house, similar to a laundry room? If there is an open plan, think about where the kitchen area ends and the living and dining areas start. This will help you think about things like overhead lighting and whether everything should be on one switch or broken up into a few zones and where those zones should be.

What Drives You Nuts?

I hate to focus on the negative aspects of anything, but it can be an extremely useful exercise if you are redoing an existing space to think about what drives you nuts so that you can come up with solutions as you make your plans for your new space.

For the messy front hall, it could be as easy as adding some hooks to the walls, and maybe a bench to tuck shoes underneath. If sound traveling through the house is an issue, maybe it can be controlled with rugs, doors, and wall hangings.

Years ago, I was talking to an old friend who often worked with my mother on construction projects. He told me that during a renovation he did at our apartment when I was in high school, my mother had him put double-thick insulation in all my bedroom walls so that she would not be able to hear what she referred to as my "Grateful Dead music."

I never knew! I would have played my music twice as loud had I known there was twice as much insulation (and, for the record, I didn't just listen to the Grateful Dead). This is a good example, though, of addressing household grievances in the design process. Clearly my mother had been bothered by the volume of my music

OPPOSITE: This kitchen in Connecticut has an attractive, useful hook on the wall by the door. The antique table is complemented by updated Windsor chairs from Design Within Reach. The flat rug is from Chilewich.

Take the time early in your project to make sure there is enough space for everything that you need to store—from linens to sports equipment, clothes, and pantry essentials. To start, measure how many feet of hanging space you have, for example, so that you can match it in the new space. If there is not enough room for storage, figure out how to expand it. Besides creating more closets or cabinets, you can add shelves and pieces of furniture that can be used for storage.

and when presented with the opportunity to solve the problem during a renovation, she took it.

I keep a running mental list of things that bug me at our house for when the time comes to fix up or redo. A few items on the list: We don't have a covered outdoor area for hanging out with friends; if we have people over during the summer, we sit in our dark living room. To take the garbage out, we have to carry it from the kitchen to the front door through the dining room, and sometimes it is drippy. Also, we have nowhere to hang a wet coat, the upstairs gets much hotter than the downstairs, and the basement is damp.

When I've brainstormed solutions, I've come up with this: I'd like to build a front porch onto the house that's big enough for a dining table; I think we would live out there in the summer. For the garbage problem, I would like to create a back door off the kitchen, but I am having trouble getting my husband to share the vision. If we had this new back door, we could put hooks on the wall next to it, which would solve the wet coat problem as well. The too-hot upstairs issue is a big one and will take redoing the heating system so there are multiple zones, and I don't know what to do about the wet basement except go down there as infrequently as possible. These things will not be addressed immediately, but I like having the list of grievances/fixes/issues ready if and when the time comes to do some work.

OPPOSITE, CLOCKWISE FROM TOP: A TV is concealed by cabinet doors that fold back. My parents' front hall closet was wallpapered (a nice surprise!) and had two shelves for storage. Antique stable hooks are decorative and keep things tidy in my front hall.

The Life of the House

As you consider your furniture plans (and scope of work), I encourage you to go deep with this idea of what doesn't work well, to drill past minor grievances and into thinking about how you live in the house. This is a moment to check in with your story and make sure you are aligned with how you want to be living in your space. Do you wish that your family had more dinners together? Would you feel less anxious if you had a dedicated workspace? Would you feel safer if you had a security system or more smoke alarms? Would you like to have friends over more often? Do you hate the color of a particular room (or your whole apartment)? What causes stress or feels lacking? Maybe you are thinking about how you can hear the toilet flush from your dining room. Maybe an image is flashing before your eyes of the front hall of your house strewn with backpacks and shoes. Maybe you can hear yourself scolding your kids for playing near a precious porcelain collection. Whatever comes to mind, write it down and then think about how it can be solved.

Part two of this is to observe where people spend time in your house. There's a lot you can learn, too, by observing how people, whether guests or family, use the space. For example, are there rooms that never get used? Chairs that no one sits in? If you have a formal dining room that is always empty, could you loosen it up or turn it into a sitting room? By analyzing the patterns of use in your space, you can start thinking about the solutions.

We have a relatively big living room that in theory should be the heart of activity in the house. I couldn't help but notice, though, that my husband spent most evenings sitting in the comfy chair in the corner of our bedroom, reading the news and catching up on things. It didn't make sense, but when I talked to him about it, he said the light in the living room wasn't good enough for him to sit in there at night and read. So, I moved the lights around, got a brighter bulb, and pleaded with him to try it again. All of a sudden,

OPPOSITE: A vintage armoire works as a bar with rechargeable LED lamps inside it. The chair is from Munder Skiles, and the pillow fabric is by Peter Dunham.

we had what felt like a new room in the house and it cost under ten dollars to get it done.

I made this point in chapter one but it bears repeating: Decorating and designing a house is not just about making it look pretty. It is about creating a space that will allow you and your family to live your best lives. Obviously, there are circumstances that you can change and others that you cannot, but sometimes a small change can have a big impact. I know for a fact that how a house is designed will help determine whether the inhabitants thrive in the space. Make your list and brainstorm the solutions; some may well only require a minor amount of effort and expense and can become part of your plan for the project. When I am working with a client, I talk to them as much as possible about what issues we could address through better design.

Blocking the Space Out

t's also time to think about which rooms, if any, will get wallpaper. Where will any wallpaper start and stop? I am always in favor of wallpapering the entire room, but sometimes there's a reason to do an accent wall or a partial room. Generally, you want wallpaper to die into a doorframe, a window frame, an inside corner, the ceiling, or something else. You wouldn't want it to stop in the middle of a wall, and it's better to avoid ending it on an outside corner, as it will be likely peel in time. By thinking about this early on, you can add a molding, if needed, before you paint, and the wallpaper can end at it.

After thinking about the wallpaper, consider whether any spaces will have wall-to-wall carpeting, or will it be bare floors or area rugs. If the wall-to-wall carpeting is in both the bedroom and the hallway outside the bedroom, is that hallway part of the bedroom suite, or should it have a different floor treatment and be treated as a different space?

Taking this time to study the actual space and block it out will help you come up with a concrete plan for the project.

OPPOSITE: The sofa fabric in this living room is the classic Brunschwig & Fils Chenonceaux pattern, the floor has wall-to-wall sisal with vintage kilims over it, and the curtain valances are trimmed and gathered—a more traditional look than if they were tailored or straight and flat.

CASE STUDY

This is the living room of my parents' old house in Locust Valley. It had a great layout with two separate seating areas. It was very comfortable and lent itself to either a family night at home or a big party. The piano bench could be pulled up to sit on; the pink ottoman was on wheels and could be rolled around. I like how there are two different armchairs at the seating area on the far side and lighting at different levels, high and low. As you work on a furniture plan for a big room, think about whether it's best to have one or two, or more, seating areas.

Things to Consider about Your Space

Spend time in your space and think about where furniture will be placed. This will allow you to think about things like what you'll see from your bed when you wake up in the morning and where the best natural light is for a reading chair.

1. Do you want to see the TV while you cook dinner? Where do you want to be able to watch TV?

2. Do you want to see the sun set or sun rise (if an option)?

3. Are there parts of the house that are particularly loud? And will that affect any work or sleeping areas?

4. Is there a view out the window that you want to embrace or avoid? If so, how will that affect how you arrange your furniture?

5. What are the sight lines from room to room? From the living sofa, will you be staring right into the laundry room?

6. Do you want to keep an eye on your kids? How does that affect the space planning? Or if you have teenagers, maybe you want them to have a space of their own.

OPPOSITE: Horizontal shiplap wainscoting is practical and pretty in a powder room; its straight lines offset the curves of the wallpaper pattern.

CONSIDERING THE ESSENTIALS
with Lilly Bunn

What is something that you consider essential to a house?

LB: While I still love to separate myself from the kitchen (I don't like to cook or see food lying around), many families want it all to happen in the same room. In a recent project (pictured on pages 112-13), I designed the room for how the clients wanted to use it. Originally a (very) formal dining room on Park Avenue, now it's got everything in one space: kitchen, dining, and comfortable seating.

What are some considerations in designing a space like this?

LB: The decorator needs to be very precise in blending soft fabrics with sticky things like food or Play-Doh. You can't get spaghetti sauce on the sofa! The perfect furniture plan is always a must. Answer all the key questions for the room at the outset: How will I use this room? What must I be able to do here? Can I see the television while I'm washing dishes (and do I want to)?

How do you start the design process? Where to begin?

LB: You have to become one with the space and really accept the space. You do this through the plans. The plans are essential.

What other advice do you have for starting a project?

LB: Find your dream home first, and then dream within those parameters. If you've got a Pinterest image of a house with an ocean view, I hate to tell you, but your small apartment in the city is not going to look like it. You need to accept what you've got and then work with it. It's like how clothing always looks better on the model.

Another thing we always do at the start of a project is photograph and measure what a client already has. Don't just throw everything away; there may be things to repurpose or reupholster. We have, for example, cut down an old living room rug to be a stair runner.

What are some other essentials for a house?

LB: Seating arrangements are so important. Pay attention to ones that you think work well and are comfortable. Take notes!

OPPOSITE: Designer Lilly Bunn used a variety of patterns that all work together in her bedroom on Long Island: a geometric on the rug, a floral on the bedspread, the woven wicker texture of the headboard, and the vertical lines on the wall.
FOLLOWING PAGES: Lilly Bunn helped a client transform a formal dining room into an open-plan multiuse space, a feat that required careful attention to the furniture plan.

CHAPTER 5

Building Your Schemes

I hate to make myself sound like a dinosaur, but . . . when I started working with my mother at her interior design business, it was 1999 and the Internet was brand new. We had one email address for everyone in the office to share—it was an AOL account and it was cutting edge. There were no smartphones to take photos. We bought and developed film. If you wanted to go shopping for a lamp, you had to actually get yourself to a lamp store and talk to a person face-to-face. Needless to say, we did things differently than we do now.

Even before the Internet, there were already so many choices to make while decorating: What color should the walls be? Should there be patterns? Should everything be smooth and shiny? Add to that now the 5,000 dining tables to consider within seconds with a Google search and you might feel overwhelmed and want to go do something (anything!) else instead of decorate.

Making Choices

The world is your oyster, but how do you make a choice when there are an infinite number of things to choose from? You create a scheme. Schemes are the collection, or grouping, of elements, from fabric swatches to paint colors, that

OPPOSITE: The walls in this cottage dining room are painted Benjamin Moore New Dawn in a flat finish. A sisal rug and antique chairs found at auction fit the country look, while the leopard-print rug on the stairs adds a dash of the unexpected.

will make up the design. Together, they will help you to filter all the options to arrive at a well-edited selection that will fit your desired story and budget and the vibe of the space being designed.

As you begin to look at specific furnishings, dedicate a tray, basket, or surface for samples and images of furniture so you can look at how they work together. This could be a mood board, or whatever works to help you to see everything together as a grouping. In general, it is a good idea to get an actual sample of anything you are considering—whether it's a fabric, a window shade, or a wood finish. If you can't get a sample, try to see it somewhere in real life. You need to touch a fabric, for example, to know how soft it is, and you need to see it with your own eyes to really know what the color is.

As you start building your schemes, think about your anchors. If your anchor is a rug, then the sofa fabric for that room should work with it. If it doesn't, find another sofa fabric. The wall color should work with it, too. And here is where the confidence comes in: you will need to develop the self-assurance to know when you think something works. Maybe I wouldn't choose it, or your friend doesn't agree, but if you think it works then it works. There isn't necessarily a right answer. Your eye has been trained by your inspiration photos, and this will help you look at your schemes with confidence.

When building schemes, it's important not to forget about the floor material, existing or new. When I start a renovation, I get a sample of what the floors will be—a wood stain, a tile, or whatever it is. Even if the floors aren't going to be finished for months, we want this sample to work with as we scheme. This

ABOVE: A Fornasetti wallpaper and terrazzo have an Italian vibe.
OPPOSITE: Examples of a variety of room schemes in progress. You can start to see the feeling and look that each room will have.

is an anchor and a decision to build upon. Is the wood floor dark or light brown? If the contractor can't make a sample for us to approve and work with in advance, I usually find a piece of wood or even a photograph that is close to what we want, and then we match it when the time comes.

The choices that you make as you build the schemes will be informed by the feeling you want the space to have. Study your inspiration images again. What materials do you see in these photos? Are the walls and furniture all light? All dark? Or a combo? Look at what you have in your scheme and think about what is missing. Maybe you will see that to get the look and feeling you want you need something made of bamboo in the room and that will direct your search. Does your inspiration photo have patterns? Then maybe you should be looking for a pattered chair fabric.

This is a process, and each decision builds on the next. It's like solving a puzzle, but there isn't one right answer. That is the fun of it.

Know What You Are Looking For

It's important to learn to say no quickly to things that don't make it through your filters. I remember that whenever I said to my mother that I loved a chair or a fabric, she'd ask, "Yes, but for where?" A chair alone is just a chair. It's the context that the chair fits into that really matters.

Knowing your space intimately and figuring out where the furniture should go will help you narrow down your options. With a furniture plan you can figure out what pieces of furniture you have and are going to keep and what things you are looking for and what size they should be. If you don't have a list of what you need to source, then now is a good time to do that. My mother used to use a red felt tip pen to put a check on furniture plans for each piece of furniture that was selected and definite. Everything without a check was what we were still looking for.

OPPOSITE: A New York library with indoor/outdoor sisal rug for practicality, chairs from Hayloft Auctions recovered in Peter Dunham fabric, and coffee table from Gracie. The four round mirrors on the wall in the corner lighten up a dark space. The walls are Benjamin Moore Iron Mountain. This is a new version of the room on page 66 taken after a renovation of the apartment.

FOCUS ON: EDITING

Decorating requires wearing the hat of an editor throughout the process—from the general questions of how the room will function and what colors it will be to the details of which chairs will suit the story and the look that is desired. A decorator acts as an editor by vetting choices for a client and putting things together into schemes. If you are doing this yourself, it will require making a lot of decisions, and for that you will have to trust yourself, be true to yourself, and think about what makes you happy.

When you shop for a sofa, instead of going down a rabbit hole and looking at three hundred sofas, you have to define at least broadly what you are looking for before you start looking. You are searching for a sofa that is 8 feet long and no more than 40 inches deep. You know this because you have studied the space and measured. The sofa should work with your story. Maybe that means it's a sofa bed because you want to have extra space for guests, or maybe it's a very comfortable traditional looking three-seater because that's the feeling and vibe you are after. Maybe you have kids and dogs and need a sofa covered in a performance fabric. If you are on a tight budget, don't spend time looking at sofas you can't afford. Don't even peek at sofas until you have first thought about what you are looking for.

Be Inspired

As you collect ideas and focus on specific colors and items, take time to clear your mind: go to a museum, tend a garden, or look at things that you find beautiful. Find quiet time where the ideas can percolate in your brain. As you meditate on the space you're building, listen carefully to your thoughts—maybe you'll think of a shop to visit, or get an idea for a wall color. Training yourself to be creative and have confidence in your inspirations is

THE PERFECT BED

For a bedroom to look finished, the bed linens need to be considered—don't forget to include them in the budget. Their colors and patterns can make (or break) the room. You need to think about the sheets; a down comforter or thin quilt, and the pillow shams; Euro-size pillows, 24 inches square, are comfy to lean against and can add a punch of color. Extras, from a row of pillows at the head of the bed to a throw across the foot, finish the look.

RIGHT: A custom-made headboard in a gray Perennials fabric with a line of pink welt across the top is dressed up with oversize square pillows and a contrasting throw across the foot of the bed. The smaller pillow brings pattern and relates to the art on the wall.

the most important part of learning to think like a decorator. Decorating isn't necessarily quick or instant. It takes time and focus to get it right. For it to be successful you have to give yourself creative space.

Finding inspiration often means making the effort to go see things in person and talk to the furniture makers, dealers, or salespeople. This was one of my mother's golden rules. We have gotten used to buying furniture online, and there's nothing wrong with it, but it is always better to see it in person if you can. And it is always beneficial to meet in person, whether it's with an upholsterer, an antique dealer, or a contractor. It will be more efficient and informative in the long run and seeing things and talking to experts in person will help you make good decisions and learn more along the way.

The key to making decisions in order to avoid being overwhelmed and the key to building schemes is to know more or less what you are looking for before you start looking. Repeat your story and the feeling you are looking for like a mantra. Study your inspiration images again and see what you should be looking for. Be open to "aha moments," like realizing you need something bright orange in the room. This could be a pillow or a painting. Unplug, and spend quiet time noodling through the project with tangible samples as much as possible. If you are feeling overwhelmed by the choices, go back to the beginning and restate your story, the feeling you want, and how much money you want to spend. Think about what you already have and what is really essential to you now that you need to source. Pick one or two photos of interiors that you want to channel for this project. Study these and get back to work on it.

OPPOSITE: Amanda Nisbet made this gracious, classic entry approachable and comfortable, yet unique for her client by combining lacquered walls, custom cerused-oak sconces, and a one-of-a kind Nisbet-designed plaster coral light fixture that was painted Yves Klein blue.

CASE STUDY

As you develop your schemes, remember that you can use the same fabric on multiple pieces of furniture. In this bedroom in our old house the chintz is on almost everything! This creates a feeling of uniformity. It's cozy, and very nice to do in a bedroom.

The Order of Operations

As in math, there is an order of operations for decorating: It's called SMO, for select, measure, and order. For example, if you want to have wallpaper in a room, the most efficient order of events is to select the wallpaper, have the person who will hang the wallpaper over to measure the space and tell you how many rolls to order, then order the wallpaper. The reason you need to select the wallpaper first is that different papers have different size patterns and roll sizes, so without that information the paperhanger won't be able to tell you how much you need.

The same is true for upholstery and making curtains. You need to select the fabric and know what style you want for the curtains before you go to the upholsterer to find out how much fabric to order or what their price will be. Again, the fabric repeats and the style of the upholstery will affect the fabric quantity and the cost of the work.

A basic order of operations is having a furniture plan or some sense of what pieces you need and what size furniture will work before you start shopping. Otherwise, you end up buying things that aren't going to work in the space.

If you are refinishing wood floors and painting and hanging wallpaper, start with the floors, then paint, then the wallpaper comes last in the finished space. There almost always needs to be a paint touch-up at the baseboard after a floor is sanded, so sand first, then have the painter in. On a big renovation the painters might paint a first coat, then the floors get refinished, then the painters come back for the final coat.

Wallpaper typically goes on last, sometimes even after the movers have brought the big bed down the narrow bedroom hallway that is getting the wallpaper. This is not some science that has to be learned and understood entirely before you start a project, but something to be aware of so you know to talk to your contractors, painters, and upholsterers about the right order of events.

OPPOSITE: The striped wallpaper in this guest room of my parents is a bold choice that works with the slope of the roofline. The mix of stripes and floral chintz fabric with gathered dust skirts makes for a cozy guest room. The rugs are flokati, shaggy wool from Greece.

FOCUS ON: COLOR THEORY

Architect and designer Nina Edwards Anker designed her house, Cocoon, around the idea of color theory, which is the study of how color evokes feeling in a space. Color theory says that blue, for example, creates a calming effect so it lends itself to a quiet place. Yellow has energy, so it is good for dining rooms. The idea that the elements of a space—from colors to lighting—can affect how you feel is something to keep in mind as you make design choices.

ABOVE AND OPPOSITE: Cocoon has translucent colored skylights over the hallway, with vermillion red, signaling sunset and rest, near the primary bedroom, and yellow, signaling zenith and activity, closest to the living room.

CREATING SCHEMES
with Katie Ridder

Are there any particular questions you ask a client at the beginning of a project?

KR: I get a game plan on how they live. Do they entertain? How formal or casual are they? I end up with a program for the project based on the feedback.

Do you have any advice for someone feeling overwhelmed by too many options while decorating?

KR: It's important to see the whole project and how each room interacts with the house as a whole. It starts with a furniture plan and understanding how each room is used. Schemes are honed, based on the feedback, and then narrowed down. We send schemes home with clients so everything can be absorbed; questions come from that and then they are further refined.

How important is it to unplug and think about the decorating off-line?

KR: I'm hardly ever unplugged, unfortunately. I find I have good ideas in the middle of the night though—and I always remember them!

Do you ever have to change course if something isn't working out as planned? Is flexibility in thinking important for a decorator to embrace?

KR: Flexibility is important, and stepping away and returning to fine-tune a day or a week later is something I always do. I revisit things all the time before the client signs on the dotted line.

OPPOSITE: Designer Katie Ridder loves to include attention-grabbing elements in entryways. In this case, she utilizes the double-height ceiling and impressive staircase to display Chinese export porcelain resting on brackets. **FOLLOWING PAGES:** Ridder set the tone for this bedroom with the boldly colored fabric by Swedish fabric house Jobs Handtryck. In general, for children's bedrooms she looks for fabrics that are sturdy but attractive, avoiding schemes that only suit a narrow range of childhood years.

CHAPTER 6

Being Flexible

At this point, finally, you have started building your schemes and buying a few things to put your decorating plans into motion. Maybe you've scheduled the painters, or found a living room rug that will be the anchor for the design of the room. You've put a lot of time and thought into it, even though it's still far from finished. And, in the process, maybe you've gotten attached to some ideas, such as having a wet bar or a king-size bed. As you start to make firm commitments, though, it's important to be flexible and revisit decisions or ideas that may have once seemed great but just aren't working anymore.

Killing Your Darlings

In my twenties, I worked as a general assignment reporter at a weekly newspaper on Long Island, and later I wrote for magazines. I always took to heart the quote by William Faulkner about the writing process: "In writing, you must kill your darlings."

I don't think it's a coincidence that many decorators are also writers or come from an editorial background. I believe it's because the creative process of the two disciplines is similar. In decorating, you also have to "kill your darlings."

OPPOSITE: This Parsons-style table in my living room is 30 inches high and doubles as a desk during the day; it can also be set up as a bar for a party. The tabletop flips open for projects that require more surface area. The ferns and the green benchtop give it life. The Japanese ceramic jar under the table was my father's, and having it around makes me happy.

FOCUS ON: FLEXIBILITY

Is there something in your plans that isn't quite gelling? If so, it might be time to step back and change course. It's easy to get attached to a plan or an idea, but it can also be a relief to let it go. Maybe something is pushing the budget, or an early decision didn't keep up with how the project evolved, or maybe you are trying to find the perfect thing when an *almost* perfect thing will do. If a room doesn't feel quite finished, don't fret; keep adding layers and accessories from pillows to throws to books on a coffee table and it will fill out.

RIGHT: This living room on Long Island is meant to be a relaxed spot to hang out with friends and family or to watch TV. The sectional seats are deep enough for a nap and with throw pillows comfy enough for a party. Natural materials in the rug, the chairs, the light fixture, and the stool tie together and add to the beachy look.

Doing this while writing might mean cutting out a clever phrase that made you happy when you wrote it, eliminating a secondary character who didn't add anything to the plot, or chopping out a paragraph that is beautifully written but over-explains something. Writing these things was part of your process, but cutting them will make the final product better and tighter. You can always keep a file of these edits for use another time in a different place.

In decorating, it's almost certain that there will be "darlings" that must be let go of to arrive where you want to be at the end of the process. The wisest thing a decorator can do is recognize and redirect when something isn't working or when something is not in line with the story, the look, the feel, or the budget. The moment when you say it out loud can be difficult, but it will be a big relief: "I don't think the old dark gray rug is working in the new space." Or, "Realistically, a king-size bed is too big for this room."

The Whole Is Greater

I was working with a client a few years ago who fell in love with a beautiful custom-made teak framed sofa and equally beautiful and expensive fabric to cover it. The sofa was blowing the budget, and if we bought it, we wouldn't have enough money left to finish the rest of the room. We were stalled. Any other sofa I showed her paled in comparison. The idea of instead

THE ALMOST PERFECT THING
The dresser in this photo was one of the first things we bought for the project. It cost thirty dollars at Hayloft Auctions. The plan was to paint it, as we didn't love its finish. But when we got the white beds, the dark blue grass-cloth for the wall, the art, and the rug together, the older looking chest gave the room some soul and we ended up leaving it just as it was.

OPPOSITE: The contrast between the wall color and the bed frames inspired the rest of this room's design. The art was perfect for the story of a beach house; we chose a white frame to continue the contrast. The dark handles on the dresser pick up the dark color in the art and help the room feel balanced.

CASE STUDY

Several years ago, my family and I moved into an apartment in the same building where my parents had lived that had the exact same layout as theirs. This was just after my mother died and I had most of my mother's furniture to use to decorate our new apartment. I loved my parents' apartment—it was beautifully decorated, very comfortable, and it felt like home. The easy thing would have been to basically recreate their apartment in our new apartment. I had to step back, though, and ask myself if I wanted to live in the past or if I wanted it move into the future and create my own look. After reflecting, I decided that the answer was I wanted to move into the future with a nod to the past. So, I kept some pieces and I sold or gave away others. I kept the sofas because they fit perfectly and I could eventually recover them. You'll see here some photos of the two apartments—old and new. The point is that it took some flexibility to rethink the space. The process took letting go of some things that I loved, such as a beautiful Regency-style writing table, the hand-painted floor cloth that I loved but that felt too formal, and the old silk lampshades that had seen better days.

ABOVE: In my mother's living room, a painted floor cloth, made of canvas, adds pattern but is still traditional. OPPOSITE: In my version of this room, a more modern woven rug and graphic throw pillows update the look. FOLLOWING PAGES: I added patterned pink upholstery to the mix, got rid of the silk curtains, and positioned a fig tree by the window for some color and life.

using the expensive sofa fabric for just pillows didn't fly. Then one day my client called me and said she thought we should get an inexpensive sofa and finish the room with haste so she could host a holiday party soon.

And I was like, hallelujah! That teak sofa was beautiful, but it did not fit the project's budget and getting stuck on it completely stopped us in our tracks. "The whole is greater than the sum of its parts," wrote Aristotle, and though I doubt he was thinking about decorating it certainly is true here. We didn't need that exact sofa to create a great room. We needed to stay focused on the whole space, not one element of it.

Context Matters

You may have your heart set on something, but the reality may be that it doesn't make sense in your space as you've planned it. My friend Lily moved to a new house and really wanted an L-shaped sectional for her living room. She picked one out that she liked, and I looked at it with her as we surveyed the space. We talked about how she wanted to use the room—she wanted it to be for entertaining and conducive to good conversations. The L-shaped sectional was going to take over the entire space. There wouldn't be room for end tables with lamps on them that you could set drinks on. We realized the room with the L-shaped sectional was going to be like a TV den and not the cheery space for conversation that she really wanted. The L-shaped sectional of Lily's dreams was not in line with the story and feeling she wanted for the space, and so she had to let go of it. She ended up getting a regular sofa, and she put fantastic red Parsons tables on either side of it—all of which together created a cozy and comfortable area conducive to conversation.

ABOVE: This New York living room has armchairs on swivels from Oomph for flexibility in the seating arrangement, and the poufs can be moved around. This is an updated version of the room on page 65, rearranged after a renovation of the apartment.

Letting Go

These are instances when you have to recognize something isn't working and decide to change course; sometimes, though, the choice will be made for you and you need to remain flexible and go with it. It's not worth dwelling on things that you can't change.

THINK AGAIN

For my bedroom in Rhode Island, I found the perfect bright blue kilim from Morocco online. I bought it and planned the room around it. Then . . . it didn't arrive. I received an email saying it was no longer available. Well, that was a bummer. I had already recovered the headboard with fabric that tied in the bright blue. I had to keep moving forward though, so I went with a white fluffy flokati rug. One day I hope to find the perfect blue rug for this room.

RIGHT: I wanted this bedroom in my country house to feel cheerful and fun, so I selected this brightly colored Schumacher fabric offset by the Moroccan pom-pom bedspread from Creel and Gow. When possible, I always like to have a seating area in a bedroom.

It's inevitable that on any big project there will be something that doesn't quite happen as expected—a rug that was selected and schemed around will be discontinued, or the new stock of a fabric will arrive in a funny color. Perhaps the pillows you wanted are sold out. Sometimes a project or a plan evolves as everyone has more time to think it through; maybe the room that was getting wall-to-wall carpeting would be better with a cork floor, or the room that was going to have a sofa and chairs would be more useful if it had instead a long table that could be used for games or projects. The point is to keep an open mind and be willing to reconsider and reselect without a lot of drama—it happens, and when things change it often makes the outcome even better.

The Home Office Dilemma

Being flexible also means repurposing spaces in your home. Maybe a guest bedroom eventually becomes an office, for example. Whatever the situation, it is important to stop and evaluate how your space is working for you and what, if any, changes you need to make in order to live your best life in the space.

I set up a home office for myself in the only place that made sense: a corner of the living room in our apartment. It was good, but I kept getting stressed out because it looked messy. Also, I was right in the middle of the apartment and fair game for anyone in my family to ask me a question, usually when I was on a phone call or doing something that required concentration. In reevaluating the set up, I realized I needed a folding screen that I could hide behind and that would conceal my desk in the evening when we wanted to use the living room for its intended purpose. I couldn't believe how much frustration and stress I went through before recognizing this solution—I wished I had stepped back and examined the situation more objectively earlier, when it started to bug me.

ABOVE: A table opposite the foot of our bed in New York can be used as a desk, but also holds some of my favorite objects that simply make me happy: my great grandmother's jewelry box, a statue of the Buddha Manjushri that I bought in Kathmandu, and the ceramic cups that my mother used as pencil holders. I find it humorous to have that little pear on the big bracket on the wall, a simple offering. The African mask came from Hayloft Auctions.

There are so many examples of how flexibility is important, but the bottom line is that it is critical to embrace and anticipate the evolution of a home and of a project and the reality that you will have to let go of some of your "darlings" to get closer to the best solution for a space. If something isn't clicking, it's usually for a reason, and there's a better solution waiting to be brought to the table.

A healthy home is not static, nor should it be—people start working from home, children grow up and their needs and preferences change. And the design process is not linear. It will take turns and require rethinking things and recalibrating when something isn't coming together. Being flexible and constantly evaluating what is working and what isn't will help you arrive at the best possible result—for now.

FLOORS

Floor material is a big consideration. Wood planks and tiles, whether ceramic or stone, add color and pattern. If you are choosing or changing the floors, think about what speaks to the local vernacular, what is practical, and what fits your budget. Wood floors can be either solid or engineered wood; in a humid environment an engineered wood floor is more stable. Factory finished wood is faster to install than solid wood but can be more difficult to refinish later on. Ceramic and stone are durable and keep cool even in hot climates, but are hard underfoot.

RIGHT: Katie Leede designed this flexible indoor/outdoor space in California. The Murphy bed folds up to allow for ample floor space. Leede upholstered the headboard in a pop of fuchsia linen for an element of surprise and comfort. The antique rug brings pattern, color, and texture to the room. It's a good idea to have at least one item with age in a room.

The Final 10 Percent

Accessories and layers give a room personality and make it look finished. You can execute your furniture plans and schemes, move everything in, and still feel like something is missing. In truth, you are only 90 percent of the way there. The final 10 percent of the decorating is transformative, which is why it is so important to leave some room in your budget for the accessories, such as books, decorative objects, and pillows.

1. A room won't look finished until the art is hung. It often takes time to find the right pieces. It's a good idea to think about art as you design the space to begin with, but it can be supplemented and tweaked. A mirror can lighten up a dark corner, for example. The moment the art is hung in a project, it starts to feel finished.

2. Tabletops and counters need to be set up with accessories, ideally of varying heights. You may have a lamp on a side table, but for the room to look finished, the table will also need a few objects, such as a small tray, a decorative box, a book, and a candle. In a bar area, you will need to set up a tray with bar accessories, a pitcher for water, coasters for wine bottles, a corkscrew, and an ice bucket. This looks nice and also makes the bar inviting and user friendly.

3. Throw pillows on sofas and beds add color and comfort. Pillows can help to tie a scheme together.

4. I always like to add a plant to make a house feel finished, whether a big potted plant that fills a corner or a small one in a cachepot on a tabletop.

5. If you feel like a room isn't working, just keep going. Add books on a coffee table, candlesticks on the dining room table, and a framed photo or two on a side table. Bring in a couple of small footstools that can be moved around. If the room needs more color, add pillows and throws.

OPPOSITE: Designer Amanda Nisbet wanted to make this hallway a destination, not just a pass-through. Lacquered deep navy cabinets with nickel inlay create fun and glamour.

CREATIVE THINKING
with Corey Damen Jenkins

How important is it to be flexible when decorating? In terms of how space is used and also in terms of the design process and recognizing when ideas might need to be reconsidered?

CDJ: I think it's imperative that people are flexible when it comes to decorating a space. As the global events of 2020 showed, our circumstances can change overnight. Rooms that may previously have received little or no use—dining rooms for example—may suddenly take on new, multiple usages i.e., as a home office, classroom, or place of study.

How can someone gain confidence for designing and decorating their own house?

CDJ: Confidence in decorating one's space comes from practice and a willingness to embrace the fact that you may not always get it right on the first—or third—try. Use your home as a laboratory to test out various concepts, color palettes, and materials. And by all means, study the work of established designers whose work aligns with your taste and vision. Illustrated books offer a wealth of knowledge.

Are there any particular questions you ask a client at the beginning of a project?

CDJ: I always ask if a client has worked with an interior designer in the past, and if so, how was the experience. What went right? What went wrong? How was the communication? Using a scale of one to ten, I also want to know how they would rate themselves as delegators versus very hands-on. There are really no right or wrong answers to these inquiries, but having that information can give me a snapshot as to how our project could unfold.

Are there any questions you think someone should ask themselves before starting a home redo?

CDJ: Always ask yourself whether you are designing in the now or for the long term? Are the selections you're making solid investments, or something you will tire of in a few years? The most timeless interiors are those that are well-considered and given plenty of time to "bake," creatively speaking. Homeowners need to take this into account as they contemplate renovations to their properties.

Do you have any favorite tips for styling a space and finishing up the last 10 percent of the project?

CDJ: My best tip for finishing up the last 10 percent of a space is ensuring you've appropriated the proper funds for finishing touches in advance. You shouldn't be figuring that out at the end—it needs to be considered from the beginning. It's like baking a cake. Cake is nice by itself, but it's oh so much better with frosting! Similarly, a room can certainly be functional, but it's the art, rugs, tabletop accessories, and so on that can take a space to the realm of wow.

OPPOSITE: Designer Corey Damen Jenkins designed the ceiling in this living room, mixing a taupe-gray base and bright white moldings. The furniture follows this clean, sculptural lead—even the vases have a sculptural character. **FOLLOWING PAGES:** Jenkins started with the finishes in this room and worked his way down, so the rug, chosen last, ended up being a synopsis of everything else. The bergères in the foreground are antiques from the early 1900s that he upholstered in white patent leather. The pair of William and Mary wingbacks offered him a rare opportunity to use a swath of lemon yellow.

CHAPTER 7

AVOIDING PROBLEMS

My mother used to say that the fun part of decorating, the part where you look at the pretty fabrics and schemes, is just 20 percent of the business. The other 80 percent is the part where you have to place orders, deal with problems, and review lots of paperwork. I remember Mom interviewing young people who wanted to get into the design business and her saying afterward that they would be in for a shock when they found out how much of decorating is really problem-solving and logistics.

On any project, of any size, there will be issues—it's the nature of the beast. With some luck and smart thinking, good planning, and vigilant oversight you can avoid them before they become consequential. What can go wrong? True stories include things from basic to mind-blowing, such as:

- The selected fabric has just been discontinued.

- The vendor lost the order.

- The item broke in transit.

- The custom-made rug is the wrong size.

- The new kitchen floor is bubbling.

- The expensive custom pillows were thrown out by FedEx.

- The wallpaper was hung upside down.

- The new icemaker is annoyingly loud.

- The floor was finished with the wrong stain, despite an approved sample.

- The piece of art that the room was designed around doesn't actually fit on the wall.

- The custom fabric was printed on the wrong color background cloth.

OPPOSITE: The front hall in my New York apartment is lacquered. I wanted it to feel like you were walking into a cloud when you arrived. The first attempt at getting the color right was a bust; it was like stepping into a Tiffany & Co. box! Luckily, I checked the sample color in person before the painters did the entire room.

FOCUS ON: DOUBLE-CHECKING

To think like a decorator is to check proposals, invoices, and estimates and all receipts on an order to make sure the information is correct.

Nothing but Problems

My mother also used to say sometimes, after a long day, that interior design was "nothing but problems." That sounds a little depressing, but the good news is that there is much that can be done to avoid issues or to resolve relatively small problems before they turn into major problems. For example, there's a big difference between the wrong tile being delivered to the job site and the wrong tile being delivered and installed at the job site. What could have been a simple return to the vendor turns into demo-ing the wrong tile off the wall and placing a new order, at someone's expense, for the correct tile.

Keeping the Peace at Home

If you and your partner are decorating together, spend extra time talking with each other about the things we cover in our first four chapters. Know your story, discuss the feeling to be evoked by the space, look at inspiration photos together, discuss what is non-negotiable, decide on a budget, and then talk about what is essential to you both. While you're at it, talk about the problems you each have with your current living situation so you can address them in your new iteration. And, of course, be willing to compromise.

If your husband has a special movie poster collection that you don't like, let him have a place for at least a few of the posters—if it makes him happy it will make you happy in the long run. And, as hard as it might be, don't roll your eyes every time you give a friend a tour of the house and get to the poster collection.

OPPOSITE: The bar in my apartment has Fornasetti Acquario wallpaper with almost-black cabinets to match the ground of the wallpaper. This allows the fish in the wallpaper to pop. I like how you can close the doors to the room and pretend you are in a fish tank, which leads to the joke people then make about getting tanked in the bar.

OPPOSITE: A checkerboard floor can be installed straight or on the bias, as it is here. In my opinion, the bias, with its diamond shapes, feels more sophisticated.

RIGHT: The wrong wall tile was sent to the job site for this bathroom; it was darker than what we selected. Catching it early, before it was cemented to the wall, made all the difference. The white chandelier is from Stray Dog Designs.

Steering Clear of Trouble

Here are a few things I've learned over time about preventing issues:

1. Items that are ordered from far away are more likely to be delayed. A company can quote you a lead time for chairs coming in on a boat from China, but they can't control whether the shipment gets tied up in customs. If you are on a tight deadline, order items that are in stock or made locally.

2. Mills and fabricators in Europe typically close for a few weeks in August. If you want something from Europe to be delivered in August or September, you need to get your orders in early enough for that to happen.

3. Always have a CFA (cutting for approval) of the current stock of fabric sent to you. If you are working with a decorator, he or she will be doing this for you. Sometimes the sample you have is not taken from the current available stock of a fabric, and occasionally there is a significant difference.

4. Document decisions in an email. No one's memory is perfect. Someone might forget what you said, or might have remembered it differently. Maybe you misunderstood what someone said. It is always a good idea to send an email to recap decisions made in person or over the phone.

5. Check in on projects regularly in person. A phone call or email with your contractor is fine, but to see things with your own eyes, on site, will help you prevent or catch problems early. Follow-up is critical. If a contractor has a question, answer it quickly. If something needs your approval, don't wait. If an order is supposed to come in soon but you haven't heard from the vendor—check in. Crazy things happen. Deposit checks get lost in the mail. Mills close unexpectedly. Delays happen, and you aren't necessarily notified about them. It's your responsibility to stay on top of things, to be cheerfully persistent, and to be an active participant at every turn.

6. When a problem does happen, be reasonable. Don't kill the messenger. Address it in a quick and appropriate manner and move on. Work with your teammates on solutions. Good relationships are essential and it's critical to be respectful, to listen to everyone, and to remain positive and productive for the best outcome.

7. Understand that good design takes time. I worry that television programs showing super speedy home transformations ruined some people's ideas of what to expect. Design work is a process, and it should move forward at a steady clip but there is no getting around the fact that the time has to be put into planning, building the right team, and getting it right. Rushing the process might make for good programming, but is not good for long-term, high-quality design solutions.

OPPOSITE: A graphic vintage Swedish rug is layered over a larger sisal rug. Layering rugs like this can allow you to make a rug you like fit better into a space. It also adds texture and interest to a room. The throw pillow is a Josef Frank design, also Swedish. The coffee table is vintage Roger Capron—an eclectic mix.

TROUBLESHOOTING
with Kristin Paton

Do you always anticipate there being problems?

KP: Yes. You always need plan A, B, C, and D. As you're putting your plan A in place, get ready to have B and C ready to go. Interior design will never go 100 percent as planned. There is so much human error that we cannot control. You always have to be ready to go with the backup plan. That's not being negative—it's just being a realist.

What is the best way to deal with problems?

KP: The best people in our industry are the ones with grit and grace. They know how to problem solve quickly without panicking—or they are graceful panickers. I always say to my team that they need to have grit and grace.

Do you have an example of something that went wrong?

KP: We waited six months for a custom dining table from England, and when it finally arrived the client, who had been upset about the delay, was standing in the window of the house watching the movers bring it in. As the guys were carrying it from the truck across the street to the house, one of the movers had a knee go out, and he dropped the table in the middle of Newbury Street. It broke into a hundred pieces.

Is there any way to prepare for trouble?

KP: If you're doing it on your own, you just need to know there will be problems. Things will get stuck in customs. Someone will mismeasure so you have to order five extra yards of fabric months into the process, or the sofa won't fit through the front door, or the rug shipped from overseas and arrived with a funny smell. There is so much stuff that goes on.

Do you have any tips for preventing problems?

KP: Double- and triple-check your shop drawings and your measurements if you're doing anything custom. Check if things will fit in the elevator or through the front door. We have everyone in our office look at documents such as purchase orders. We triple-check yardage. When you hire a designer, they are doing all that for you. Part of why you hire a professional designer is to mitigate issues.

What can be done to help keep things on schedule?

KP: When we order things with long lead time, we put it on the calendar to check in once a month with the vendor, and then as it gets closer to delivery we check in once a week.

Any ideas to keep things moving smoothly?

KP: Pick your team. Whether it's your upholsterer, or your curtain people, you want to stick it out with the same team. They are there for you through the good and bad. You want your core team so that when you need a favor or something has gone wrong you have someone to call. Don't spread the work out over ten workrooms; stick with your team.

OPPOSITE: This powder room in Brookline, Massachusetts, designed by Kristin Paton, is a great example of high/low design. The vanity base and basin are mail-order pieces that then were painted tortoiseshell by a decorative painter. The silk hand-painted wallpaper is from Fromental, the mirror is from Carvers' Guild, and the stone was handpicked from Cumar. **FOLLOWING PAGES:** This dining room by Paton needed a refresh. The alternating dining chairs add pattern. The dark walls, starburst ceiling light fixture, and vibrant blue curtains create a feeling that is both sophisticated and comfortable.

CHAPTER 8

Understanding Suitability, Simplicity, and Proportion

In her book *The House in Good Taste*, Elsie de Wolfe wrote that the three essential tenets of interior design are "suitability, simplicity, and proportion." My mother had a postcard with those three words hanging on the bulletin board over her desk. I love the idea of boiling good design down to three directives. Maybe a designer known for maximalism would have said the three tenets were "color, texture, and make it a double" (and the book probably would have a different title!). But these three tenets from Elsie de Wolfe are excellent and serve as the pillars of classic interior design. Let's dive in them a little more deeply.

Suitability

I understand suitability to mean two things. The first is whether a material is literally suitable for the job you are going to give it. For example, it wouldn't be suitable to upholster a family room sofa with a thin silk fabric. The silk would fall apart quickly. The second part of that is the idea of whether something suits the intended look or feeling of a space. The look of a thin silk fabric would be far better suited to a low traffic formal room. It would help convey a feeling of delicacy and luxury.

OPPSOITE: We wanted to keep the design for this Long Island house light and timeless. The butcher block, wood floors, and white backsplash all work to this end. The clean shape of the light fixture suits the story as well, but its metallic lining adds a chic exclamation point.

Simplicity

Simplicity is the best advice ever. Just keep it simple. The best result is usually the most straightforward. Be Zen. It's advice for decorating and for life. This idea can be interpreted in different ways. I see it as meaning sometimes a basic white slipcover or a plain white ceramic tile is the best solution. That you don't need to try to be "fancy" at every turn, or make your interiors cluttered. Simple, straightforward layouts and designs are often the best.

Proportion

Proportion is more difficult. It is about training your eye so the scale of the furnishings and architecture work together. Some furniture is just too big or too dinky in a space. My husband inherited a captain's chair from his father, and when we brought it to our house it looked like a chair on steroids compared to the other things in the room. We had to either decide to live with it or rehome it, but there was no way to fix the issue. Proportion means reading the fine print detailing the measurements before hitting buy on that website. You might love a certain lamp, but before you get it you need to consider its size and how that will work with the table it's going on and the other furnishings in the space.

Sometimes, you want to have something out of proportion in a space, say a big thing in a small room, but it should be done

CASE STUDY

This was my mother's bedroom in New York City, a comfortable, quiet oasis. The custom headboard with a gathered border is upholstered in chintz, with matching ruffled pillows. The bracket, which is in my bedroom now (see page 149), with the traditional Chinese ceramic foo dog helps to fill the wall and finish the space. A wall mounted lamp is a great space saver. This Marshall Field-style chair is particularly nice for a bedroom. Its tight, tufted back is not too deep and it fits well in a corner.

OPPOSITE: My mother's bedroom was so peaceful. The colors are muted, everything looks soft. Having an off-white wall-to-wall bedroom rug makes it feel light and clean.

"Your ability to edit things comes from your experience and confidence and also your ability to say 'yes' and 'no' to things. There aren't just two ways to do a room, but rather twenty-two ways to do a room. At a certain point you have to make up your mind. If you want to do a room in peach and beige, then that's what you should do. You have a vision—you have to be confident in your vision. Decorating is emotional, and you have to keep this emotion alive as you design a space."

—*Kirill Istomin*

RIGHT: A sitting room on the Côte d'Azur by designer Kirill Istomin channels 1950s modern, California style, with pale blues, creams, and grays. Furniture is by and inspired by twentieth-century design icons William Haines and Karl Springer. The table lamps are custom-made by Christopher Spitzmiller and the sconces are custom from Thomas Boog in Paris. All this together creates a mood of relaxed glamour.

purposefully and with intent. Having a tape measure handy and checking everything will do much to help keep the proportions of the various pieces in the room hanging together.

Akin to proportion is balance in a room. Balance is about weighing the various pieces and colors going into a space and making sure they hang together as a whole. Balance doesn't mean symmetry necessarily. If you have a room with muted colors, it might feel out of balance to have one screaming hot pink chair. Maybe it would feel balanced to have two hot pink chairs and a deep saturated color on pillows on the sofa.

Achieving balance takes study and thought during the planning stages of the design process. It takes looking at your schemes and samples all together and considering them carefully. Do the colors and textures speak to one another? Balance can also be tweaked at the end with styling and accessories. Achieving a balance that works for you takes trusting your eye. There should be equilibrium in a space. It can all be intense, it can all be quiet, or it can be a terrific combination of both. Take the time to look at your schemes, the samples, the photographs of furniture for the room and ask yourself if this feels balanced. Is one part of the plan looking like too much or too little, too hot or too cold, too timid or too bold?

These are all additional filters to run selections through. They are more subjective and can be more challenging to get the hang of than the filters we spoke about earlier, such as what's the story, the feeling, the essentials, and so forth. Mastering these requires studying interiors that you like while considering suitability and proportion of the furnishings. Most importantly, it requires confidence and knowing what you like.

OPPOSITE: Our house in Rhode Island is a mix of modern and traditional. I like how the white Verner Panton Barboy offsets the antique campaign table we use as a bar in the living room. The Barboy is from my first apartment shown on page 17. I bought the film reels from a friend who was having a moving sale because I liked them; they have leaned against a wall in every house I have had.

"Sometimes you're in a rush to get things done, but if you sense a hesitation in yourself, it's often better to wait. Sometimes patience is really important, and if you don't have an answer or the perfect thing right now, have faith that it will come to you."

—*Katie Leede*

RIGHT: Katie Leede used a large-scale artwork to open up this bedroom. Such pieces serve as windows into another world.

FINDING YOUR STYLE
with Kirill Istomin

How would you define style?

KI: When your own eye and confidence get together that is when style is born. Your style is the way you compose the world around you. It's your own vision, the way you see things and the combination of things. When we say "style," we obviously have the assumption it's chic or outstanding, but it doesn't have to be. Style is one person's vision. Style is not buying something that's been preselected for you. You have to have guts to have style.

What role does proportion play in interior design?

KI: Again, it's your own eye. It's about something big next to something small. People often don't look at the measurements and the sizes of things. They buy objects out of context and they don't think how they will fit proportionately on the wall or in the room. When proportion is right it looks beautiful. Sometimes when a room looks a bit boring, the proportion is too right. When it's too perfect, it's boring. This takes us back to style, which isn't about being perfect but about being yourself.

How do you consider balance as a designer?

KI: Like music is a composition and a piece of art is a composition, interiors are also a composition. Color and textures are aspects of the composition. I have clients who are nervous about things not being symmetrical. I have to convince them that one thing may not be symmetrical but the overall space has balance.

Where do you find inspiration for your designs?

KI: Instagram is a beautiful thing. It's an instant source for lots of visuals. I personally have over 150,000 photos in my phone and iCloud. I take photos of everything—the store window and the colors they put together; the ad in the magazine and how they put things together. I have a lot of books, lots of historical materials. I love the history of interiors, and I follow a lot of people on Instagram. Fashion inspires me.

Inspiration is everywhere. Lots of people may see what I see but not everybody is actually going to think about this particular detail or combination. The details I see can be translated into something modern, or can be translated into a pair of curtains for my work. You have to have a trained eye and be willing to see the details. You have to zoom in. Your mind has to be trained to zoom in on the details of an image and translate it for what you are creating.

OPPOSITE: This penthouse dining room designed by Kirill Istomin has custom wall panels with inserts in Edelman leather, a custom chandelier designed by Istomin (inspired by a 1910 design by Adolf Loos), and dining chairs by Baker upholstered in Opuzen cut velvet. The ceramic plate on the wall is by Pablo Picasso. Istomin designed the custom wool and silk rug, and the collection of glass vases was purchased at Christie's. **FOLLOWING PAGES:** The living room of the same penthouse was inspired by Istomin's mentor, Albert Hadley, and design legend Jansen. The wool and silk rug is custom-made by Stark, the pair of brass and steel table lamps are vintage, and the coffee table is custom-made with a top made from Edelman leather. The sconces over the mantel are by Bella Figura and the art is *Beautiful Mickey* by Damien Hirst.

CHAPTER 9
HAVING CONFIDENCE

Confidence and style go hand in hand, whether in decorating or life in general. Having style takes confidence. Having confidence gives you style. With confidence and a solid point of view, decisions are infinitely easier to make. Knowing what you like is the biggest game changer in design. If you aren't sure, if you find that you are constantly second-guessing yourself, then spend some more time looking at photographs and thinking about it. My mother and I used to enjoy critiquing rooms, talking about what we liked and didn't like about them. We didn't always agree—there isn't always one right answer. It's more about having a point a view. If you are at a restaurant, or even a friend's house, think (to yourself!) about what you would keep and what you would change. What would your constructive criticism be? It may not be exactly what you want to do in your own home but it's good training to think about what you would do differently to that space. I am always mentally rearranging the furniture wherever I go. The best, though, is being in a room that you realize is basically perfect, where you wouldn't change a thing.

OPPOSITE: Nothing says confidence like color. Here, designer Katie Ridder combined a bold palette with a flexible seating plan that includes a deep-seated sofa and chairs, as well as more portable furniture that can be scooted around as needed. **FOLLOWING PAGES:** Designer Kirill Istomin created this "casual collectible" home in New York's Chelsea neighborhood for a young family who collect important design and art. The homeowners didn't want to compromise their sophisticated style for the kids, so Istomin's design mission was to marry refined taste with the needs of a young family.

> "The only real elegance is in the mind; if you've got that, the rest really comes from it."
> —*Diana Vreeland*

Style

One of the biggest compliments my mother would give someone would be to say: "She's got real style." I came to realize this meant the person had confidence, knew what she liked, and demonstrated as much through her choice of clothes, decorating, and her manner. This was the holy grail. I remember being in church with Mom once and the fashion designer Carolina Herrera was there a few pews up on the other side of the aisle. It didn't matter to Mom what the priest's sermon was that day—the lesson of note was that Carolina Herrera had real style as she sat there in church, impeccably dressed with her hair just so.

Carolina Herrera is quoted as saying: "I don't like trends. They tend to make everyone look the same." You could say that anyone has style who has a solid point of view and compiles an interesting and unique assortment of elements around them. Other people may not love it, but it's your style. When Mom and I were writing *The Pocket Decorator*, we included a sidebar that said: "Having style is not buying the entire furniture set where everything matches, but rather it is putting together a collection of your own pieces with your own point of view." And I think that still sums it up.

OPPOSITE, LEFT: Designer Lilly Bunn combines striking tiger stripe pillows with a vivid pattern on her slipper chairs.
OPPOSITE, RIGHT: A bold vintage felt target captures your attention in a guest room on Long Island.

Confidence

Confidence typically comes from experience, but also can be cultivated by spending time and effort to develop your point of view. Whether you are a professional designer, a client, or designing for yourself, cultivating confidence and a point of view is essential.

I think that confidence is best illustrated through example. There is a photo of Diana Vreeland, the legendary *Vogue* editor, in her apartment that I love. It embodies confidence. From the color, to how she's sitting, to what she's wearing—it's wholly original. She worked with decorator Billy Baldwin to create a "garden in hell." That was her idea, and he worked his magic to make it happen. I personally would not want to live in that red room, but look at her there. She owns it.

THE POWER OF BOLD

When you pick paint colors, don't just think about the wall color. Consider how the trim and ceiling colors work with the wall color to create the look you want. Dark walls with white trim have a graphic look. When the trim is painted the same color as the walls, it is quieter. Paint it all red for great effect. The trim can also be a dark color, as in the photo on page 92. Study your inspiration photos and be confident about doing something bold or unusual. I love to paint ceilings pale blue, though a pale pink ceiling can warm up a room. Be bold!

RIGHT: Designer François Catroux's apartment in Paris from the July 1976 *Architectural Digest* is one of my favorite rooms. I love the contrast of the walls and trim. It's comfortable, elegant, modern, and timeless all at the same time. It reminds me of my childhood, in a good way.

When you look at this photo (see page 194), you don't suppose that Vreeland hemmed and hawed over what to wear, or whether the room really should be quite so red. I don't suppose she was thinking at the moment this photograph was taken: Am I wearing too much red lipstick?

Gloria Vanderbilt is another example of someone who created some truly fantastic interiors. Maybe they are an absolute inspiration to you, or maybe they are not your taste at all, but whatever you think of them, they exude confidence. I don't imagine that she was wringing her hands and hoping it wasn't too much or wishing she had played it safe.

Trust Yourself

I have said throughout this book that it's important to study your inspiration photos and to use them to help you decide on the look you want to achieve and to train your eye. Studying and getting ideas from inspiration photos is very useful as you develop your own point of view. The critical part is to have the confidence to run with it and use those images as a launchpad for creating your own unique space that will reflect who you are and how you want to live.

It's always great to talk about your plans and ideas with someone whose opinion you value; that is part of what a decorator does for a client. Having someone else weigh in can be comforting and can lead to new ideas. At the end of the day, though, you have to make your own decisions.

Having confidence in your decorating doesn't mean that you have to go over the top and do something wild—though you could. Having confidence is about trusting your vision and your instinct. It's saying no to things you don't like without apology. It's knowing what you do like and not second-guessing yourself unless proven wrong. It takes the same amount of confidence to have an understated and quiet interior as it takes to have a bright red living room. If you waffle on a decision, noodle it through and sleep on it—then make your decision and stick with it.

OPPOSITE: This is my parents' dining room in New York City. The walls, trim, and wall-to-wall carpeting are all deep red. The dining chairs are a yellow velvet. The room was a nighttime room, a little exotic, and a great setting for a dinner party. Talk about confidence!

MAKING A STATEMENT

Covering the furniture, curtains, and even the walls of a room in the same fabric creates a striking, cozy environment. You just have to be darn sure you love the fabric. Using a toile—a French print—everywhere in a guest bedroom is one of my favorite ways to do this. You can find prints that come in both fabric and wallpaper. Doing this takes confidence, as you have to be willing to go for broke on one fabric design. You have to commit and fully embrace it.

LEFT: Diana Vreeland's New York living room designed by Billy Baldwin with the directive that it should be a "garden in hell" has a chintz sofa and walls.

"
Gloria Vanderbilt was incredibly brave and confident. Gloria wasn't asking her friends what they thought. It's good to have a sounding board, but sometimes if you ask for a friend's advice and they say, 'No,' you have to go ahead and do it anyway if it's something you want."
—*Christopher Spitzmiller*

ABOVE AND OPPOSITE: Gloria Vanderbilt had a wonderful, confident decorating style. There are multiple patterns, quilt patterns on the walls and everywhere else, and plenty of color. Her rooms show so much personal vision.

CONFIDENCE
with Alexa Hampton

Any ideas for how someone can boost their confidence when it comes to design?

AH: There is a philosophical way to boost confidence and that is to remind yourself that, while your house is in one sense an object that you look at and so there is an objective consumption of it by you and perhaps guests, it is, more importantly, a habitat. You are in it as well as being of it and if you can only judge the success of your interiors based on what your sister-in-law is going to think, then you will ultimately have lessened the amount of joy you're going to derive from it. So, you have to remind yourself that this (your rooms and your ability to design them) is an indulgence; it's a total privilege that I get to do this just for me. Perhaps I'm being selfish or self-involved, but the result will make me happy and functional and a better citizen of the world. If that notion doesn't give you confidence, then at the very least it should empower you.

What do you ask your clients at the beginning of a project?

AH: You ask them, "What do you love? What do you hate? What makes you comfortable? How are you going to use the house?" I would add to those questions: "How do you wish you lived?" Because ambition in this way can be conflated with confidence and can lead to a successful outcome.

There is a lot of ambition in my apartment about who I wish I were. And I'm aware that it likely creates some cognitive dissonance for any innocent observer who sees my very buttoned-up living room and then sees me walk in barefoot, wearing my Gap T-shirt and jeans. They might think, "I don't understand how these two things go together." But I don't care—it makes me so happy to sit in my living room in my Gap T-shirt and my jeans with my hair in a topknot, all the while looking at statues of Caesars and interior photographs of the Vatican. They fill me with nostalgia, they fill me with happiness, they speak to my better angels—not the schlump on the sofa.

Ambition is important. If somebody is informal but they don't want to live in the kitchen, and they love, in their fantasy, to be seated at dinner every night with their family, then give them that dining room. In having that you learn to live with it and you learn that it may not be so out of reach. Likewise, maybe you don't have to be so precious to have it. It's a kind of a confidence to know that you deserve what you want.

How important is it to be original when designing?

AH: I find originality and being true to yourself stylistically are almost diametrically opposed because if you are trying to be original there is an attendant anxiety about doing something innovative and unprecedented. Very few people are able to develop their aesthetic sense without precedence. Certainly, my life is all precedence. I've been

OPPOSITE AND FOLLOWING PAGES: Alexa Hampton's Kips Bay Designer Show House bedroom from 2012 was painted in Benjamin Moore Dragon's Breath. The desk is from Florian Papp, and the bedside tables are from Objects Plus in New York. The pleated bed skirt and canopy and the fur throw all contribute to the elegant, classic, and luxurious look. Embroidered fabric is from the Alexa Hampton line for Kravet.

lucky to be steeped in the history of beautiful rooms. The result of that exposure is that I can ask myself how I want to progress from them. What do I revere? What do I jettison?

When there's a miasma of hovering anxiety about being an "original," then you can frequently end up with three-legged chairs. That kind of originality is not always pretty and, quite frequently, unsound from an engineer's point of view.

I much prefer the idea of finding the style that you love best. It definitely will have moments of uniqueness, but you don't have to mint a new style everywhere you go. You can reference or quote these great rooms that you've seen because they had a huge impact upon you.

Where do you find inspiration?

AH: You've got to see it. You've got to travel, go to museums. Fashion designers are given such license to take their craft seriously, to say, "I'm being inspired by this canvas. Let's turn it into a dress." I think there's so much that is practical about a designer's job that we don't always feel that license to be purely artistic. I think we should take that license. We should feel comfortable doing it.

When I hear a designer complaining that their clients just want, for example, "a boring white room," I bristle. I, for one, can open Pinterest and find four hundred amazing white rooms. Surely, you've got a great white room in you. You've got to say to yourself, "I'm going to make the coolest white room anyone's ever seen."

You've got to get into it and get excited, and that has everything to do with whether it will be successful. You can call that enthusiasm confidence. You've got to psych yourself into being confident about it so that you can be unabashedly invested in the outcome.

RIGHT: Details from Alexa Hampton's Kips Bay Designer Show House bedroom from 2012.

CHAPTER 10

Celebrating the Everyday

The goal of a decorating project should not be the final photos on Instagram; rather, it should be the life you'll live and the happy times you'll have in the space once the project is done. A lot of the decorating comes together in the last 10 percent as you hang pictures, accessorize tabletops, fill bookshelves, and actually start to live in the space. The decorating project will eventually end, but there will be, or should be, an ongoing effort to breathe life into the house. It's the part where you set the table for dinner with some consideration for how it looks and how it makes you feel; the part when you put flowers on your front hall table, and decorate for the holidays. I think of these final and ongoing touches as creating happy moments in a home.

Be Your Own Stylist

After my mom died, I kept hearing from her friends that they remembered her for how she celebrated the everyday. She made pancakes on Saturdays; she lit the candles for dinner; she sometimes had a friend over for tea, which meant getting out her nice plates along with the funny old teapot and tea cozy.

OPPOSITE: A glass top on a coffee table allows more of the rug pattern to be seen. Fresh flowers are essential to everyday happiness, as are an assortment of favorite objects: a brass tray, red lacquer incense holders, a silver box, and a favorite book.

OPPOSITE: I love to set the table at our house in Rhode Island. It is absolutely worth the effort to have the cloth napkins, the placemats, and the colorful glasses—it makes dinner at home feel like a special occasion. **RIGHT:** I always use these traditional Spanish wine glasses, maybe because I imported them from Spain and had to retrieve them from cargo at JFK airport in the middle of the night (a good lesson in reading the fine print).

THE OCCASIONAL TABLE

When space allows, I like to have a small table to sit at for dinner that is outside the kitchen, ideally in a living room. In my house in Rhode Island, the table is by the fireplace, which is cozy in the winter and still works well in the summer. We have squeezed three people around it for dinner, and played back-gammon and done puzzles on it. If we have several people over, I rest a tray of cheese on it.

RIGHT: The back wall of the bookcase in our Rhode Island living room is painted Benjamin Moore Chili Pepper. This is one of my favorite tricks for adding color to a room without it being overbearing. The color is a back-drop for the items on the shelves.

FOCUS ON: THE DETAILS
This backsplash is a brass laminate that was much less expensive than real brass. I like the warm reflection. If you have a bar, bring out the nice glasses. You can find them at auction if you don't have any. A brass tray is a very useful and attractive accessory for a bar or tabletop. If you see a brass tray, buy it— you won't be sorry.

She had joy and enthusiasm for the flourishes of her everyday routine that made a nothing-special day feel memorable. She worked hard, so it's not like she had all day to set the table. These were small and often quick gestures, like buying a rosemary plant for the kitchen or fussing with what was on the coffee table. The lights were dimmed for dinner to create the always important "ambiance." She cared deeply about the details, which is at the heart of what a decorator does.

When working on photoshoots at the end of a project, there is often a stylist there who helps get the flowers and plants in the right place, who nudges the bookshelves into order for the photograph, and who perhaps suggests hanging something on a wall that looks empty. I adore working with a stylist, as it brings new energy and a fresh set of eyes into the last part of a project. At my own house, I try to be my own stylist on an ongoing basis in an effort to make my home feel more alive.

OPPOSITE: Flowers bring color and life to a room, making it festive even if you are home alone. If you are going to a friend's house, it's always nice to bring a small bouquet of flowers.

What Makes You Happy?

It's important to have things that make you happy around a house, whether it's two colors next to each other that give you a thrill or a shell on a side table that you brought home from vacation. This goes back to our first chapter; it's celebrating your story and how you want to live. If you wanted to have bridge games at your house, then do it. Set the bridge table and make a date. If you wanted family dinners, then light the candles, dim the lights, and make it feel like a special moment.

Things and spaces in the house that are sad, stagnant, broken, cluttered, or unused should be brought back into circulation or eliminated. The old dusty plates that were your grandmother's? Get them out and use them. The cut-crystal bowl? Fill it with ice and shrimp and invite a few friends over. Some people care more than others about these details, but to think like a decorator is to keep a constant effort going to make a space feel vibrant, happy, and comfortable. A home is alive. It evolves, and it should support the inhabitants in living their best, happiest, and healthiest lives possible. It doesn't have to be expensive or fancy—it only needs to be well considered, comfortable, and able to set the stage for the story of how you want to live.

"A happy moment for me is having in a TV room a basket of matching blankets so everyone in the family gets one. I also like having bright yellow umbrellas; I got the idea from Kate Brodsky." —*Lilly Bunn*

"In every aspect of your home, all five senses should be addressed. All senses inform your experience. Don't forget greenery. Use pretty napkins. Elevate the everyday. Get the table set. Every night at dinner time, I light the candles, even if it's just me. It's not a big deal and it makes it feel a little nicer."
—*Amanda Nisbet*

"Every night I light the candles for dinner. Especially with our kids on machines all day, it's the one time of day we see each other. It's important to set the mood, and candles do that. If someone is in a bad humor, the ritual of lighting candles lifts the spirit."
—*Nina Edwards Anker*

OPPOSITE: A dressing room in Providence, Rhode Island, has matching wallpaper and fabric on the window treatment. The smaller print on the stool was existing and works well with the larger scale pattern.

Creating Happy Moments in Your Home

Think about areas of your house that are cluttered, unused, or congested and attack them. Clear them out, empty them, and put something that feels fresh and vibrant in the space, even if it's nothing but open air. Here are some ideas:

1. Create a centerpiece on your dining table—it could be a bowl of lemons, a pair of candlesticks, a small plant, a few stones. Find something amusing, seasonal, or just pretty. Wing it or look through some inspirational photos of tables that appeal to you.

2. Try to have at least one thing that makes you happy in every room, no matter how small or simple. A framed map of a place you love, a family photo, a throw in your favorite color, for example.

3. Even if just a small succulent, bring plants into your home.

4. Look at your bookshelves and see if you can improve them. Check your inspiration photos for ideas. Find some objects you love—a pair of foo dogs or a plate—and work them into the bookshelves. Get rid of books you don't want and make room for new.

5. Examine the lighting in your house. Are there bulbs that are too bright? Are there dark corners? Are people working in the dark? Troubleshooting the lighting can make everyone happier.

6. Are the lampshades sad or frumpy? Changing out the lampshades can make a big difference. Is the lining ripped on any of the fabric ones? Are some of them so bright white they don't go with the rest of the room? A new vanilla colored paper shade can make a big difference.

7. Set the table for dinner. Use the cloth napkins—they don't need to be ironed. Light the candles. Create a moment.

OPPOSITE, CLOCKWISE FROM TOP LEFT: A few things that make me happy: Duck decoys and old blue glass wineglasses. Cut flowers in a bedroom. The colors and combination of this wallpaper and Indian miniature print in my apartment. A tabletop at Christopher Spitzmiller's Clove Brook Farm that creates a happy moment with accessories.

FINISHING TOUCHES
with Christopher Spitzmiller

How do you accessorize in your house?

CS: Accessorizing for me is more about editing than selecting. I accumulate things and rotate things in and out. Christmas is my reset. I strip everything down then and redo everything but the lamps.

Is your house ever finished?

CS: It's completely a work in progress. I have a pair of ancestor portraits that always hung next to each other, then I bought fifteen of Mario Buatta's spaniel portraits. So, I moved the ancestors to the other wall to make room. I don't always want to look at the same thing. Things have to change. As with flowers—peonies, tulips—there's a season for everything.

What are your recommendations for finding the right lamp?

CS: It's important to vary the landscape of a room; Albert Hadley used to say that. You want to have lights at different levels, not all on one level around the room. When sitting, you don't want to look up and see the bulb and electrical parts. You need a shade that covers them, and also the table and lamp need to be the right height.

What inspires you?

CS: I get inspiration seeing what's out there. I love looking for things. I'm an antique and auction junkie. It's a constant hunt. Even if I don't buy things, I get the inspiration to make things and reproduce shapes.

I shop online, too. There are things you can't get to see in person. I have had good luck shopping online, but sometimes you miss something online. Your own eyes seeing something in person are the best tool, and also making relationships with dealers is key. In person, you can say, "Hey can you watch out for this thing I'm looking for?" In person is important. Don't hesitate to pick up the phone and call someone.

Any tips for setting a dining table?

CS: Bunny [Williams] has a trick to set the table with flowers and some sort of ornament. I set the table with John Derian's ladybugs, or frogs, or honeybees. I like to have little objects around; they add a nice element of surprise.

OPPOSITE: Christopher Spitzmiller shows his green thumb with plants on stands in the windows. On the desk is one of his handmade lamps in green with a fabric lampshade. FOLLOWING PAGES: Christopher Spitzmiller's dining table is set with flowers from his garden and homemade flatbread (left), and a corner of the living room features the best accessory of all—a dog (right).

COLLECTIONS

This corner of Christopher Spitzmiller's living room is a wonderful example of creating an interesting moment with a collection. Here he celebrates his love of dogs with the dog portraits he purchased from iconic decorator Mario Buatta's estate, as well as ceramic dogs displayed on brackets. A gallery wall like this offers a fantastic opportunity to display a passion.

RIGHT: Christopher Spitzmiller's living room in Millbrook, New York, has so much personality, with its peacock-blue corner banquette flanked by portraits of his ancestors on one wall and dogs opposite.
PAGE 223: A dusty pink bed from Crate & Barrel, a colorful pink, blue, and yellow area rug from Wayfair, custom curtains and valances, and a vintage hanging light fixture give this New York bedroom a cheerful and airy feel.

ACKNOWLEDGMENTS

I am so grateful to so many people for their time, encouragement, and expertise in making this project come to fruition. Kathleen Jayes, our editor for *The Pocket Decorator* and *The Pocket Renovator*, made this project possible. She encouraged me to pursue it and worked with me on the vision for it and she has been an editor extraordinaire along the way. I am so grateful to Doug Turshen and David Huang for their incredible design skills and all the hard work they put into creating this book.

Lily Malcom, my best friend and a book expert, was incredibly helpful with big-picture and nitty-gritty advice.

Working with photographer Max Kim-Bee was such a pleasure. I will never forget our first shoot during the pandemic lockdown when the world was standing still. Frances Bailey, Anne Foxley, Genie Trevor, and Lela Williams did wonders with styling various photoshoots and making those long days fun.

I am so honored to have such an experienced and excellent group of designers come on board to share both their expert advice and photos of their work as examples and inspiration to show how it's done. Alexa Hampton, Tom Scheerer, Corey Damen Jenkins, Katie Ridder, Kirill Istomin, Christopher Spitzmiller, Katie Leede, Amanda Nisbet, Lilly Bunn, Nina Edwards Anker, and Kristin Paton: Thank you!

I am incredibly lucky to have such great clients who have not only let us into their homes to take photos but who have entrusted us with their projects. None of it would be possible without you.

Last but not least—my little family, my bedrock, has cheered me on and given me the time and space to work on this for the past couple of years. William read chapters and made valuable edits and my daughter, Harriet, has helped me keep my nose to the grindstone. Though Harriet swears she will never, ever be a decorator, she has been extremely helpful and encouraging to me in the process of writing this book on decorating.

First published in the United States
of America in 2023 by
Rizzoli International Publications, Inc.
300 Park Avenue South
New York, NY 10010
www.rizzoliusa.com

Foreword: Alexa Hampton

Cover: Clarence House "Crosby Stripe Red 13466-04." See more at clarencehouse.com.

Endpapers: Fermoie fabric design "Marden." See more at fermoie.com.

Reverse of endpapers: Fermoie fabric design "Hamble." See more at fermoie.com.

PHOTO CREDITS:
David Banker, pp 13 top left and right; 58, 76, 107, 126

Michael Biondo: pp. 50-51

Jacqueline Clair: pp. 6, 96-97, 98-99, 110, 189 left

Steve Freihon: pp. 9, 199, 200-201, 202, 203

Oberto Gili/Condé Nast Archive, Architectural Digest © Condé Nast: p. 54

Caylon Hackwith: pp. 128, 129

Pascal Hinous: Le Style Contemporain, Architectural Digest © Condé Nast: pp. 190-191

Horst P. Horst, House & Garden © Condé Nast, December 1, 1977: p. 55

Horst P. Horst, Vogue © Condé Nast 1979 pp. 194-195 and June 1, 1975 pp.196, 197

The Ingalls: pp. 214 bottom left, 217, 218, 219, 220-221

Stephan Juillard: pp. 181, 182-183

Max Kim-Bee: pp. 2, 5, 14, 20-21, 23, 24, 25, 26, 27, 29, 30, 32, 34, 35-36, 39, 40, 44-45, 47, 71 bottom, 85, 86-87, 88, 90, 92, 94, 101, 102 bottom left, 104, 108, 109, 114, 116, 117, 119, 120, 122-123, 125, 134, 136-137, 139, 141, 142-143, 145, 146-147, 149, 152, 159, 160, 163, 165,171, 176, 189 right, 204, 206, 207, 208-209, 210, 211, 214 Top left and bottom right, 223

Francesco Lagnese/OTTO: pp. 74-75, 79, 80-81, 82, 83

Adam Kane Macchia: pp. 186-187

Peter Margonelli: pp. 71 top, 72-73, 102 bottom right, 140, 162, 173, 193

Poul Ober: pp. 17, 19

The Eames House interior photographed by Mitsuya Okumura. © 2022 Eames Office, LLC. All rights reserved: pp. 52-53

George Mashall Peters: p 13 bottom right

Eric Piasecki/OTTO: pp. 130, 132-133, 184

Ali Price: p 13 bottom left

Chip Riegel: p. 213

Mark Roscams: pp. 43, 65, 66, 68, 102 top, 214 top right

Kelsey Ann Rose: pp. 112-113

Eric Roth: pp. 166, 168-169,

Durston Saylor, "Interior Design Legends: Mark Hampton," Architectural Digest © Condé Nast: pp. 56-57

Werner Straube: pp. 155, 156-157

Tim Street-Porter: pp. 48-49, 150-151

Lesley Unruh: pp. 61, 62-63, 178-179

Simon Upton: pp. 174-175

ART CREDITS:
p. 182 © 2023 Estate of Pablo Picasso / Artists Rights Society (ARS), New York

pp. 182-83 © Damien Hirst and Science Ltd. All rights reserved / DACS, London / ARS, NY 2023

Publisher: Charles Miers
Senior Editor: Kathleen Jayes
Design: Doug Turshen with David Huang
Production Manager: Kaija Markoe
Managing Editor: Lynn Scrabis

Printed in China

2023 2024 2025 2026 / 10 9 8 7 6 5 4 3 2 1

ISBN: 978-0-8478-7294-7

Library of Congress Control Number: 2022945690

Visit us online:
Facebook.com/RizzoliNewYork
Twitter: @Rizzoli_Books
Instagram.com/RizzoliBooks
Pinterest.com/RizzoliBooks
Youtube.com/user/RizzoliNY
Issuu.com/Rizzoli